The
TEN PRINCIPLES
from
EL CANTARE

VOLUME I

IRH Press

BOOKS

IRH PRESS

New York

ISBN 13: 978-1-942125-85-3
ISBN 10: 1-942125-85-2

Printed in Canada

First Edition

The
TEN PRINCIPLES
from
EL CANTARE

VOLUME I

RYUHO OKAWA'S FIRST LECTURES
ON HIS BASIC TEACHINGS

RYUHO OKAWA

IRH PRESS

Contents

CHAPTER ONE

The Principle of Happiness

CHAPTER THREE

The Principle of the Mind

CHAPTER FOUR

The Principle of Enlightenment

CHAPTER FIVE

The Principle of Progress

Preface to the newly revised first volume of
The Ten Principles from El Cantare

This book compiles the five lectures that I gave in 1987, the year Happy Science began its activities. I was 30–31 years old at the time.

Until a few years ago, I could not read the lectures because I was embarrassed about how young my level of enlightenment was.

This year 2020, I, at the age of 64, am the World Teacher, and Master and CEO of Happy Science Group with shojas (temples), branches, missionary centers, and others in over 107 countries* throughout the world. In Japan, there is no other religious leader like me.

A total of 10 lectures that I gave within the two years—1987 and 1988—compiled in two volumes, will surely be beneficial in passing on clear records of Happy Science's history to future generations.

The DVDs of these lectures are also available. I hope you will experience the spiritual power of my words through them, as they are so much more powerful than the printed words.

Ryuho Okawa
Master & CEO of Happy Science Group
July 26, 2020

---

* At the time of original publication. As of October 2021, Happy Science has members in more than 164 countries.

Preface to The Principle of Happiness*

It was in the spring of March 1987 when I gave the first public lecture for salvation at the Ushigome Public Hall in Tokyo. I introduced the "Principle of Happiness" with a burning desire to save humanity. There are four principles—love, wisdom, self-reflection, and progress—to become happy, and they are the modern Fourfold Path.

It is not an exaggeration to say that the path of Happy Science for these past four years was predicted in this first public lecture. So I can strongly say to you that this is a must-read, must-have book for every seeker of Truth.

The lecture, "The Principle of Love," is a declaration of the Savior that predicts the coming of a new era under the spiritual guidance of Jesus Christ. In "The Principle of the Mind," I have taught how far you should explore the mind as you practice the exploration of the Right Mind, and this is a must-read for people who are studying the teachings of Happy Science.

This book filled with my passion is for those who have the same desire and who have been eagerly awaiting its arrival. Now is the perfect time for this book to be released. Now is the time we must win.

Ryuho Okawa
Master & CEO of Happy Science Group
September 1990

Preface to The Principle of Enlightenment[†]

Attaining enlightenment is very hard. But remember that you can experience true happiness only when you have passed this severeness to attain enlightenment.

People are in fact very spiritual. When you leave this world, the only thing you can take with you to the other world is your mind. So enlightenment, which is the happiness of the mind, is all and everything. Don't think that you are happy when you have not developed spiritually or experienced a true awakening, for without these experiences, your happiness is only an illusion.

This book, *The Principle of Enlightenment*, which I preach to all people, is the eternal Truth that shall be passed on. This is the voice of the Eternal Buddha. Listen to this passionate and powerful speech.

Ryuho Okawa
Master & CEO of Happy Science Group
October 1990

---

[*] The title of the book published in 1990, containing Chapter 1 "The Principle of Happiness," Chapter 2 "The Principle of Love," and Chapter 3 "The Principle of the Mind."

[†] The title of the book published in 1990, containing Chapter 4 "The Principle of Enlightenment," Chapter 5 "The Principle of Progress," and Chapter 1 of Volume II "The Principle of Wisdom."

CHAPTER ONE

The Principle of Happiness

Happy Science Launch Commemoration Lecture
The First Public Lecture of 1987

Originally recorded in Japanese, on March 8, 1987
at Ushigome Public Hall in Tokyo, Japan
and later translated into English.

1

Early Adulthood

Six years ago, on March 23, 1981, I suddenly began receiving revelations from the heavenly world. The first one came from spirits belonging to the Nichiren School of Buddhism —namely, Nikko (1246-1333) and Nichiren (1222-1282). These spirits suddenly started sending me spiritual messages.

Four or five years before that, when I was still 19 or 20, I was an ordinary university student without much interest in spiritual matters. In those days, however, when I was on a bus or a train, the word ETERNITY would often appear in big white letters before my eyes. I did not know why I kept seeing the word eternity, but it would happen from time to time. Without any idea of what lies ahead, I would often say to my friends, "In the future, I would like to leave behind thoughts that will be handed down for two or three thousand years." I was not aware of why I was saying this, but I had a vague dream of becoming a philosopher or at least doing literary work. Now I understand that at that time, preparations for my future had already begun.

During my days at the University of Tokyo, I became absorbed in reading books on a wide range of subjects rather than pursuing a major field of study. But as time passed, my dream started to waver. Although I was attracted to the concept of eternity and the word eternity kept appearing in my mind, I was gradually influenced by my friends whose aim was to achieve worldly success. I then became interested in law, the law which governs society, and was unknowingly drawn to worldly success. Gradually, my wish to get ahead and succeed in the world became stronger and stronger. Because I had entered a prestigious university, I thought about how satisfying it would be for me if I could get a job that people hold in high regard and spend my life working there.

At that time, I had two options. One was to stay in the academic world and become a scholar, perhaps to specialize in political philosophy. The other was to achieve success outside academia. I continued to waver between these two paths. As graduation day approached, I still wished to pursue academia. But as I watched many of my friends attempting to put their abilities to the test in society, I was drawn to have a career outside of academia.

In university, I majored in law and studied very hard. However, I faced many roadblocks. At the time, I could not figure out why. My classmates did not seem to have any trouble finding careers in their chosen fields. In my study group of six people, everyone but me was successful in becoming a diplomat, high-ranking public servant, or legal professional. Around the time of my graduation, I was also drawn toward such a path. But for some reason, whenever

I took a vocational exam or tried to get a job, something happened to block my way at the last minute; it was as if a wall appeared in front of me. For some odd reason, obstacles prevented me from advancing in the direction of my choice on each occasion. I did not realize why this was happening to me.

I became confused and doubted if I really should get a job. However, one autumn day, I received a phone call from a trading company asking me to come for an interview. Later, I was treated to dinner and was courteously asked to come and work with them; everything went so smoothly that before I knew it, I had accepted their offer. In those days, I was still not sure of the direction I should head in. Although I had a burning desire within me, I was uncertain which direction I should channel this feeling toward. It was no surprise that I could not find a position that matched my ideals at that time because no profession would have fulfilled my yearning for eternity.

However, fate was cruel; despite being brought up in the countryside and having no desire to go abroad, I began to work for a company involved in international trade. Soon after, I was sent to work in the United States. The living environment I was in was opposite to that of Buddhist or Christian seekers of Truth. It was a dog-eat-dog world where people were pursuing results day in and day out. First thing in the morning, I would get a cup of coffee and skim through newspapers for the latest economic and financial information or for useful information that no one else knows about. I would go to the office an hour or two earlier than the other employees to read the telex messages sent from overseas, which often amounted to more than 30 feet of paper. I would analyze them and consider the strategy to solve the problems as quickly as possible. That was my work in the trading house.

2

The Path to the Truth

Despite all this, I encountered a crucial, decisive turning point in my life. It was quite shocking to me. To put it simply, I was struck by a strong ray of light—revelations from heaven revealed that I was on the wrong track for the course of my life. However, I had to make a living. After receiving revelations from the heavenly world, I knew I would not be able to continue living an ordinary life. But in the modern world, I couldn't possibly live on offerings, like the monks of old times. So I wanted to somehow balance my business career and the world of the Truth. While working in the business world, I still had a desire within me. General trading companies demanded extremely stressful work but also paid high salaries. They probably paid much better than other companies did. The trading house I worked for offered enough salary that even a young employee like me could afford a new car with a single bonus. This was the reality, and I could not easily give it up at the time.

Over the next four or five years, I continued seeking the Truth while still working in the company, but it occupied less than 10 percent of my time, or perhaps about 1 to 2 percent of it. And once every few months, I would meet with Saburo Yoshikawa (who later became the honorary advisor of

Happy Science; d. 2003) to record spiritual phenomena and discuss them. But even though these spiritual occurrences were happening all around me, I was passive in getting them out; I let him do all the work. Now, we have published eight volumes of spiritual messages, but as you can see, they are published under the name Saburo Yoshikawa. At that point, although I was continuously receiving spiritual messages, it was still uncertain what lies ahead, so I decided not to take any action until I had a clear vision of the future.

Also, I felt I was still too young and inexperienced to stand and speak in front of people. Even now, it has only been a few months since I turned 30 years old. At the time, I thought, "The spiritual phenomena I am experiencing must be real, but if I start to teach people about them now, I will surely fail—people will probably label me as a strange or insane person within a year and I will stray from my path." After all, I knew I had to compensate for my lack of experience with patience and diligent efforts. So, I decided to wait patiently until I gained the confidence to teach people the Truth correctly. I thought I should be patient and wait until the time was ripe without taking any action and believing the time for me to make a move would surely come before long.

Since then, I have accumulated many kinds of spiritual experiences. We have published books of spiritual messages from just dozens of spirits (at the time of this lecture), but the number of spiritual phenomena I have experienced over the last six years amounts to tens or hundreds as many. I have had contact with hundreds of high spirits. For my first book, *Spiritual Messages from Saint Nichiren*, I spent four years accumulating conversations with him, which means there are a hundred times as many messages in addition to the contents of that book. That book has such a solid foundation. I was determined not to make any move forward without first establishing a solid foundation for our movement.

Most people would have started preaching as soon as they received messages from Saint Nichiren and possibly would have formed a new religious organization within the year. I guess the spiritual guidance of Saint Nichiren alone and the publication of 10-20 books of his spiritual messages would have attracted several million followers in a few decades.

However, I felt what was happening to me was far more serious. I realized that Saint Nichiren was only a guide or a facilitator, and behind him was a group of over 500 high spirits who were ready to support me. Then, three or four months after my first spiritual communication, I received messages from Jesus Christ. At first, Advisor Yoshikawa did not believe me; he said it was impossible. So, I performed a spiritual message session before his very eyes. That is how our numerous conversations with other spirits began. Nevertheless, it was at least another three years before I finally confirmed that the messages from Saint Nichiren were genuine.

3

The Responsibility of a Religious Leader

Nowadays, there are many newly established religious organizations, and most of their founders start preaching as soon as they experience spiritual phenomena, taking them as the work of divine beings. However, in truth, becoming a religious leader comes with great responsibility. A simple mistake can not only mislead millions of people in this age, but also the people of future generations. The damage cannot be settled easily.

At this time, I have not announced where many of the founders of new religious groups have gone after death, but I know their whereabouts. Many people would be shocked if I were to release this information, so I will refrain from doing that, but I will release spiritual messages from the founders who have gone back to the higher realms of the heavenly world. If you do not find the spiritual messages of certain founders, you will know why.

Although I have received requests from members of several religious groups to publish messages from their founders, I do not think it is a good idea. No publisher would want to publish their messages because all they say is, "It's pitch black. I can't stand it. Help me." It would only make the readers go crazy. I cannot help but pity those founders who fell to hell after they died. It is very difficult to save them. They are aware of the mistakes they have made, but even if they correct their thoughts, that alone will not enable them to return to heaven. This is because their successors are still actively spreading their wrong teachings to millions of people. The founders pray desperately for their successors to stop, but sadly, it does not happen; they continue working diligently on behalf of their founders. The wider their organizations grow, the greater the suffering of their founders in hell. They do not stop, contrary to the founders' wishes.

The successors nowadays might express gratitude to the founder by saying, "Founder, thanks to you, our membership has increased tenfold." But this makes the founder even more desperate. The founder in hell thinks, "Now I will have to stay here ten times longer. Instead of 200 years, I will have to suffer for 2,000 years. I'm afraid I might forget that I was ever human." This is a sad case, but we cannot save them so easily even if we wanted to. Why not? In the case of usual stray spirits, I can send them to heaven after talking with them for a couple of minutes or an hour at most. But this is not the case with founders of misguided religions. They are responsible for misleading millions of followers who still believe in their wrong teachings. Unless they solve this problem, they cannot return to heaven. Therefore, they certainly would have been better off if they had moved to the countryside and grown vegetables instead of becoming founders. The worst that could have happened to them would have been to fall to hell for speaking ill of their neighbors. In that case, they would not have had to stay so long in hell; they would have been able to return to heaven relatively soon.

Now, I am giving lectures and introducing spiritual messages from figures such as Saint Nichiren and Jesus Christ, but if they were false, then I most likely will never be reborn into this world; I will not be able to return to heaven. It will be even worse for me if Happy Science grows and spreads wider internationally. Through spiritual contact with many religious founders, I learned to be very cautious. This is why I refrained from taking action until I could confirm the authenticity of Saint Nichiren with certainty. For over four years, both his messages and his character were consistent. The messages were so logical and inspiring that no living intellectuals could hope to deliver the content of a similar level.

On the other hand, spirits from hell are inconsistent. No matter how skilled they are at tricking people, their inconsistencies eventually come forth. Usually, evil spirits are straightforward; they only complain of their pain, so it is easy to distinguish them. However, the Satan or demons that possess religious founders are very experienced and quite shrewd. They show off their religious knowledge on, for example, karma or reincarnation. They may even say, "Save people. This message is God's voice, so you must spread this message to the people. Publish my messages as a book and deliver it to each and every house." Even so, you need to be cautious.

As I wrote in the booklet, *How to Protect Yourself from Evil Spirits*, it is important to have intellect or knowledge. Some evil spirits have strong spiritual powers or willpower, but because there is no school in hell where they can learn the Truth, they do not have a systematic knowledge of it. Spirits in hell who used to live as esoteric Buddhist monks, for example, would know a lot about the esoteric teachings. In particular, there is a monk of esoteric Buddhism in Japan who some people believe he restored the esoteric Shingon School and, in a sense, was more respectable than the founder of the esoteric Shingon School, Kukai (774-835). But after his death, he fell to hell and is currently possessing some religious founders and deluding people. He has extensive knowledge of esoteric Buddhism, so people with average intellect cannot see through his true nature.

If you humbly study not only Buddhism but also a variety of religions, such as Christianity, Shinto, Confucianism, and Taoism, along with ethics, science, and philosophy, and you have grasped the "golden thread" that runs through their arguments, you will be able to find their inconsistencies.

In contrast, those who believe exclusively in, for example, esoteric Buddhism or a particular sect of Christianity and who keep their eyes shut tight against other ideas can easily be deluded by entities like Satan who are experts in that particular belief. You may come across these sorts of believers in certain new Christian sects. I have often been accosted by people trying to sell the Bible on the street. Sometimes I think of giving them a copy of *Spiritual Messages from Christ*, but that might stir even more trouble. So, I always said, "I know the Bible is precious, I already have one at home." There was a time when I came out of a subway station and a woman came up to me and asked, "Could you spare me a moment?" Upon seeing me being reluctant to say "No," she said, "You seem to be troubled." [*Audience laughs.*] Of course, I was troubled—I was wondering how I could escape from her. She continued, "Perhaps you are possessed by a bad spirit. I can purify you if you can spare a couple of minutes." As I declined her offer to be purified on the streets, she said, "Why don't we move somewhere quieter?" I was at a loss for what to do. If she had purified me, she would have been shocked, so I did my best to decline her offer. But she would not give up and insisted that she must save as many lambs as possible. Eventually, I had to ask her to let me free because I believed in something else.

Having observed new religions and seen their founders in the afterlife, I strongly resolved not to tread the path of religion unless I took it seriously. I decided that even if it took me several years, I would not take any steps to appear in public until I could positively confirm that the spiritual messages I received were from Saint Nichiren and Jesus Christ.

4

Starting from Scratch

Happy Science has been prudent and careful in its exploration of the Truth. Usually, no one would wait six years after receiving messages from Saint Nichiren or Jesus Christ. People who experience such encounters would start spreading the word immediately, but I did not. I waited until I was convinced of their authenticity. My books of spiritual messages represent only one percent of all the knowledge I have acquired. They are carefully selected messages that I have analyzed from every angle and confirmed to be true.

For the first couple of years, high spirits used expedient means to communicate with us because we were not as enlightened as we are now. Because we were not familiar with the world of spirits, they guided us little by little using words we could understand. Then, after a while, they took us to a higher level. Now, after six years, we realized that we were at a very low level in our first couple of years.

This is a funny story now, but here is an episode regarding a dog we owned at my parents' house six years ago. Every night, the dog would bark furiously, so I asked Saint Nichiren, "Is there an evil spirit possessing our dog?" He kindly replied, "Yes, there are two snake spirits. That's why the dog is barking so furiously. He's quite annoyed."

Looking back, I feel sorry for Saint Nichiren. Due to such a low level of spiritual awareness I had to ask him trivial questions. This is where I started. That is what I mean by "starting from scratch." I started as beginners, just like all of you.

Now, what would have happened if we had published this in our books of spiritual messages? What would you think if we published spiritual messages from him that read:

Q: Saint Nichiren, I have a question. Our dog keeps barking at night. I don't think this is natural. He might be influenced by an evil spirit. Is he possessed?

A: Indeed, two snake spirits have possessed him.

It would be too late for us to retract this later on. As you can see, it takes two or three years for a person to develop his spiritual awareness. This applies to everyone and anyone. Only after going through this immature stage can one proceed to the next level.

There was a religious founder who passed away about 11 years ago, in June 1976. We published a book of his spiritual messages for the first time in December 1986, and it attracted a lot of attention. Now, he is back in the spirit world, but he is not at peace. When he was alive, he started his activities soon after experiencing spiritual phenomena. That was when he was around 41 or 42 years old. At that time, he was told that he would only live to 48, so he had an urgency to conduct his activities.

He conveyed the words of spirits he had written or heard, but the truth is that it is quite difficult to do this in the first few years of spiritual activity. I can say this based on my experience. Until the receiving side develops enough spiritual awareness, high spirits use expedients to convey their messages. They need to use expedients and help us, who live in this world, raise our spiritual awareness little by little; otherwise, we will not understand. No matter how great a guiding spirit you may be, once you are born into a physical body, you have to start from scratch. That is why you need to wait three or four years to get used to spiritual phenomena and confirm whether they are using expedient means or not.

I have been talking to the aforementioned religious founder for five or six years, and he told me many times about the confusion within his group in its early days. He now wants me to straighten things out by publishing several books of spiritual messages from him. However, when we try to correct his thoughts for him by publishing spiritual messages from him, his disciples refuse to believe them. "Our master's thoughts cannot be wrong, so Happy Science must be trying to change them for the worse. It must be the work of Satan." That is how they think. This is how difficult it is to make changes later on. Even if the founder gives mistaken messages early on, his disciples cannot understand that they are anything but correct, so they strictly follow his original words as a golden rule.

Early on in his religious career, he focused on the topic of Buddhism. He also spoke about the teachings of Moses, but he did not talk much about Japanese Shintoism or the Chinese philosophies of Confucianism and Taoism because he did not have much interest in them. For this reason, he thought that the eight million gods of Shinto were spirits of the sixth dimensional Godly Realm (now called Light Realm).

Some of you might wonder, "The Godly Realm is the sixth dimension? The seventh dimension is called the Bodhisattva Realm and the eighth dimension is the Tathagata Realm, so shouldn't the Godly Realm be higher? It doesn't make much sense." The religious founder himself seemed to believe that the eight million gods of Shinto were sixth dimensional spirits. He did not think highly of Confucius, Mencius, Lao-tzu, or Chuang-tzu, either. He thought this way because he did not care much about them. For example, I do not think he talked to Amaterasu-O-Mikami or the Sun Goddess. He believed that because Japanese Shinto gods were only performing purification rituals, Shinto was not spiritually advanced and that Buddhism was of a higher level. But this was all because he was running out of time.

His claim that Shinto gods were beings of the sixth dimension is now causing his disciples trouble. When I revealed the fact that some Shinto gods are very high in spiritual grade, his disciples became confused. They think, "Shinto gods aren't supposed to be very high, but they give quite advanced teachings. What's going on? I don't understand. Confucius and Mencius are supposed to be sixth dimensional spirits, but at Happy Science, Confucius is a ninth dimensional being. I can't believe this."

The point is that religious leaders must bear a heavy responsibility. They are free to speak on what they found to be true, but as for the knowledge they have yet to confirm, they must stay silent until they do so. This is why, although I still have much more to share with you, I have not released them.

I would like you to understand our standpoint. We want to build a firm foundation before we start to teach the Laws. Those who have joined Happy Science are required to explore the Right Mind daily. But some may have already forgotten about it, even if they were inspired by it when they first joined. This was exactly what I spent doing for the first six years; without exploring the Right Mind daily, it would be impossible to communicate with the high spirits. There are no exceptions to this because it is a rule. One must have the same spiritual vibration as the high spirits if one wants to communicate with them.

5

What Is a Prophet?

Quite a few of my readers might be followers of Seicho-no-Ie (lit. "House of Growth," a new Japanese religion), so in this section, I will talk about prophets. Recently, we published *Spiritual Messages from Masaharu Taniguchi*. Some executives of the group seem to think, "Based on our teachings, God does not work through mediums. Since Reverend Masaharu Taniguchi (the founder of Seicho-no-Ie) is a high spirit near God, he can't possibly come down on a human being. If he was a lost spirit, perhaps that's possible, but given that he is back in a higher realm of the spiritual world, he can't work through a human. It's impossible." They think this way because they only know one aspect of the Truth. There is no theory at Seicho-no-Ie that explains the difference between a medium and a prophet.

Listen to me carefully. They are correct in that God does not work through mediums. God does not descend on people who make a living as spiritual mediums. However, God does work through prophets. They convey the words of God.

One example is Moses, who fled from the Egyptian Pharaoh Merenptah and successfully led the Exodus some 3,200 years ago. Moses heard the voice of God named

Yahweh from heaven. To be precise, this God was a divine spirit of the ninth dimension. Moses could hear that voice because he was a prophet. It was his work and mission to convey the words of God.

Elijah was another prophet who lived about 2,800 years ago. Alone, he confronted 500 priests of Baalism on Mount Carmel to defeat their mistaken belief in Baal. The worship of Baal was a belief that satisfied earthly desires. Misguided priests taught that Baal would always grant people whatever they wished for. Elijah, who believed in Yahweh, challenged the priests to prove who God really was and said, "I believe in the one and only God Yahweh. Then, let us battle to see which is the true God, your god Baal or my God Yahweh."

The confrontation on Mount Carmel started early in the morning. Five hundred worshipers of Baal built an altar and prayed to Baal to ignite it by sending fireballs from heaven. They prayed to Baal from 9 a.m. until noon, but there was no answer—there was no fire from heaven. Believers of Baal were baffled. They thought, "This can't be happening. Baal would never forsake us." It was after 2 p.m. when they became exhausted and finally began to slash themselves with swords and dance about while covered in blood. They continued slashing each other with swords and praying aloud, "Please bring down fire," but still no fire appeared. The 500 believers prayed till 3 p.m. On seeing this, Elijah mocked them, "Then, I will pray to my God, Yahweh." He was only in his mid-twenties, which was young, and he was also jealous of them. Elijah began to pray. No sooner did he pray than fireballs or burned stones roared down from the sky onto his altar, setting it ablaze. Finally, the 500 priests of Baal were executed under Elijah's order. In the past, there were times when extreme measures had to be taken. Elijah was indeed a prophet.

Regarding a more recent time, Jesus Christ was also a prophet. Please read his words carefully. When Jesus was asked by some people, "You say, 'The Father in heaven sent me down,' but where is the proof that there is the Father or God in heaven? Show us." To that, Jesus answered, "The Father in heaven cannot be shown to you as if taking something out of a bag. But the words I speak are not mine. The Heavenly Father descends on me and now speaks." Christians do not understand the meaning of these words, but I do. The truth was that the Great Divine Spirit (El Cantare) came down and spoke through Jesus. Other high and divine spirits such as Yahweh, Moses, and Elijah preached through Jesus, or rather, they gave him inspiration when he preached. That is why Jesus used to say, "Believe my words. Those who hear my words hear the voice of God because He has come and is now speaking." Jesus was conveying God's words. Therefore, he was a prophet and not a medium.

Muhammad was another prophet. He was a merchant in Arabia. When he was 25 years old, he became ill and poor and eventually collapsed on a hot sunny day, as he had nothing to eat for days. Then, a beautiful widow, around 40 years old, leading her caravan, passed by and told her people to help Muhammad. For three days he received her care and finally recovered. He stayed at her house for a while and eventually married her.

One morning, at around five o'clock, Muhammad had a dream. In it, he walks up a hill near Mecca and finds a cave. In the cave, there is a shovel, and as he digs a hole, he finds the treasure. The dream was so clear and vivid that he decided to confirm it. He sneaked out of the house while his wife was still sleeping and looked for the hill he saw in his dream. As he approached the outskirts of Mecca, there he saw the same hill that was in his dream. Walking up the hill, he found a cave, just like the one he saw in his dream.

Muhammad went inside the cave and eventually sat down. Before he knew it, he fell asleep because he had left very early in the morning. That was when he heard a loud voice echo throughout the cave, "Muhammad, this is Allah." He was astonished. Allah was the God who appeared in the Torah or, more specifically, the Book of Genesis in the Old Testament. He thought that he heard the voice of the God of Creation and was surprised. Then, he realized the significance of this spiritual experience. By the way, Allah is the same being as Elohim (El Cantare).

So he went back home, and without telling anyone anything, he took 40 days' worth of food with him to the cave. There, he struggled for 40 days. He received revelations from Allah and messages from Gabriel; Allah taught him over a few sessions, and after that, Archangel Gabriel worked as a messenger to follow up on the specific details of the Laws. This is how the Quran—the teachings of Islam—was put together. The Quran is a book of spiritual messages, similar to what we are publishing now. Muhammad compiled God's words. But because there was neither a tape recorder nor anyone to take shorthand for him, he listened attentively and memorized the messages, word for word, every day, and had someone else record them (it is said that Muhammad himself was unable to write).

Throughout history, high spirits have been born as prophets to convey God's words. Now, we are in the same position. But just as there were no complete teachings in the past, our teachings will never be enough, however hard we may try to bring them to completion. As for the Truth beyond my understanding, unfortunately, I am unable to preach it to you. You are studying the spiritual messages of high spirits, but they are all within my scope of understanding. I have a slightly higher level of understanding of the Truth than the words written in the books of spiritual messages; however, as for the things beyond my abilities, high spirits cannot speak on them through me. There is such a limit.

6

First, Explore the Truth;
Then, Study It and Convey It to Others

I have talked about how careful Happy Science has been in exploring the Truth and the way of thinking that lies at the root of it. As I will explain in the Principle of Happiness in the next section, at Happy Science, we place great importance on knowledge because, without it, one cannot distinguish right from wrong. This knowledge is not the sort of knowledge needed for school exams, but it is knowledge of the Truth. If you examine existing religious teachings and philosophies against the knowledge of the Truth found in our books, you will find some inconsistencies. This means that our books contain certain tacit criticisms.

After all, knowledge is power. Today, there is a religious leader (Hogen Fukunaga, the founder of Ho No Hana Sanpogyo, who was later arrested for fraud) who says, "Get rid of the head." It might be a good idea to do so if your head is filled with wrong ideas, but a head filled with the knowledge of the Truth is to be valued. Socrates, for example, possessed great knowledge of the Truth, so it would be a tremendous loss to remove his head. So, as the first step, I would like you to acquire the knowledge of the Truth. Studying the Truth is the first step at Happy Science.

Some of you who joined Happy Science recently might have seen the exam for the upcoming seminar and thought, "Oh, I can't do this. It's too hard. I should cancel my membership." You might also think, "But before I do, I'll go see Ryuho Okawa. I can quit after that." I am sure people will see our exams and harbor different opinions, but this is what I want to say: We spend hundreds of hours making one book of spiritual messages. That is how much energy it takes to publish one book. What is more, the time spent on collecting knowledge that serves as the foundation of these messages is several or dozens of times longer. So, I spend hundreds of hours making one book. (Author's Note: This is what I used to do early on when I was recording spiritual messages as proof of the spiritual world.) How long does it take you to read one book? Quick readers may finish reading it in two hours, and slow readers may be able to do so in 10 hours. Some of you might have read it three or four times. That is fine. However, the time we spend to make one book is dozens of times longer. This is how we are absorbing the Truth.

When you read the books of Truth, please do not be satisfied after reading them just once; it is important to check and see whether you have assimilated what you have read. If you want to deepen further your academic studies, you can find many teachers in the present day, but there is nowhere you can go to check whether or not your understanding of the Truth is correct.

Of course, we will spread the Truth throughout the world. As I did for the past six years, I place importance on making our foundations solid. Our basic principle is to "First strengthen the inside and then the outside" or to "Build the foundations and then the pillars." So, I want you to study the Truth before you convey it. You might say you want to convey the Truth, but what will you be conveying? Our publisher is already marketing our books by printing advertisements in newspapers. That is good enough. To convey something, you must study it. And even before that, you must explore it. The correct order is: exploring the Truth, studying it, and conveying it to others.

Our organization is not yet firmly established, nor do we have our own facilities (at the time of the lecture). At this stage, it is no use spreading our books far and wide by simply saying that we have published new books of spiritual messages. This should not be regarded as true missionary work. If people think the messengers of Truth are out of their minds, it's not good. Instead of saying so, I want you to first study the Truth thoroughly for a few years, just as I spent six years creating the foundations of Happy Science. Consider carefully what you want to convey. As Jesus Christ said, "If a blind man leads a blind man, both will fall into a pit." You should not tell others what you have not understood.

New religions today often create problems because those who have not yet attained enlightenment try to enlighten other people and draw them into their organization by force. They try to subdue you or solicit you. You can find many of these people everywhere. This also happened to me about three times. It would have been fine if they were enlightened. If someone with a wonderful personality, much knowledge, and mastery of the Truth came up and talked to you, you wouldn't hesitate to give them some monetary offerings if what you heard was good. But usually, this is not the case; they try to drag those who are trying to escape to join their religion by force. I certainly don't like such behavior, and I'm sure you would feel the same way.

So the Truth must first be explored and studied before it can be conveyed. I want Happy Science to remain patient and be a group that studies the Truth for the first couple of years. We will naturally grow, even if we do not put much emphasis on doing so. Many people are asking to become Happy Science members now. Based on my estimate, we will probably grow to 4,000 or 5,000 members by the end of this year if we accept everyone. However, we do not yet have any lecturers to teach newcomers, so expanding our membership at this stage would only give rise to confusion. I think it would not be wise to start branch offices throughout the country with only me going from place to place and giving lectures. So, in the first few years, I would like to cultivate people who have enough knowledge of the Truth and can teach it to others. In other words, I want to train lecturers who can teach others and become the core of our missionary efforts. Many members are eager to start branch offices, but first, I would like them to understand fully what the branch offices are for and the content of what they will convey to others.

We have now published 10 books (over 2,900 books as of October 2021), but these are just the beginning of the foundation. We are simply telling you that such spiritual phenomena can occur and that such a spiritual world exists. Here on out, we will be teaching the real Laws. I am now building the foundations for teaching the Laws. So before you think of conveying anything, please study. To explain what I am saying now in Buddhist terms, "Hinayana (Small Vehicle) comes before Mahayana (Greater Vehicle)." Only after you have attained enlightenment can you save others. When people start doing the opposite, tragedy occurs in religion. So find happiness for yourself before trying to make others happy. From Hinayana to Mahayana—this is the correct order.

Happy Science has just started its activities. We are still at the Hinayana stage of Buddhism. I, of course, cannot wait to start the Mahayana movement and spread the Truth all over the world. But "Hinayana comes before Mahayana." I, myself, have not attained ultimate enlightenment, so I am not confident enough to preach advanced teachings to people. This applies to you, too. What did you learn from our teachings? Unless you can answer this question, you cannot teach people the Truth. (Author's Note: Happy Science began its period of great missionary work three years later.)

A member in South Korea is eager to publish *Spiritual Messages from Christ*. It has already been translated and is ready to be published. I can understand this desire to spread it, but I want us to control it for now. I hope you will understand the meaning of what I have said so far (as of October 2021, Ryuho Okawa's works including *The Laws of the Sun* have been translated into 37 languages, and Happy Science has members in more than 164 countries.).

7

The Principle of Happiness

Finally, I would like to address the main theme of this lecture, the Principle of Happiness. There are numerous ways to become happy, but the kind of happiness we seek is happiness that carries over from this world to the next; it is not the sort of happiness you can only enjoy in this world. We are exploring principle of happiness that apply to the past, the present, and the future.

The starting point of these principles is the attitude to explore the Right Mind. What is the Right Mind? Every individual has the same divine nature as a tathagata within him or her, and this is the Right Mind. I am saying we should explore it. You may think that highly developed spirits are better than lower-level spirits—for example, that tathagatas of the eighth dimension are greater than bodhisattvas of the seventh and that bodhisattvas are better than the spirits in the Light Realm of the sixth dimension. However, you should not judge people by their spiritual level alone.

The diamond within everyone is essentially the same; the only difference is in the level of refinement and the brilliance of the diamond, which is the result of numerous incarnations. Those who have made efforts to polish the diamond within have become guiding spirits. So, if you continue to refine your inner diamond, it will surely shine. This is true for everyone. However, no one can become a tathagata instantly. Your diamond will not suddenly shine; to make it shine brightly, you have to make constant and tireless efforts to polish it. These efforts are exactly what we consider as the exploration of the Right Mind; this is the spiritual discipline that allows you to discover your true nature. Through this daily effort to explore the Right Mind, you will enter the next stage in which you seek true happiness through the Principle of Happiness.

Love—love that gives

The first principle in the Principle of Happiness is "love." This love is not the kind of love that you expect to receive from others. The love that I teach at Happy Science is "love that gives." What is "love that gives"? Is it the act of giving people money? No, it is not. The true nature of "love that gives" comes from awakening to the fact that you and others are one and the same—that all human beings are children of God who split off from Him. You and others might seem completely different, but your true nature is one and the same. This is the basis of true love. It is because you think you are different from other people that friction and discord arise. Once we awaken to the fact that, essentially, we are all children of God and we all originate from God, we naturally come to love one another.

What exactly does it mean to love others? It is to wish good for others, to wish to nurture others without expecting anything in return. It is a selfless love, detached from personal desire. Because your essence and the essence of others are the same, you are required to love others just as you love yourself.

It is easy to love ourselves; we love ourselves without being taught to do so. But unfortunately, once we are born into a physical body, we forget to love others. This is why I need to teach "love that gives."

Another word that describes "love that gives" is mercy. The teaching of love sounds very Christian, but "love that gives" is the same as mercy, which is the basis of Shakyamuni Buddha's teachings. Translated into modern terms, Shakyamuni taught, "Start by giving love." This was the meaning of his teachings on mercy. So, love is the first principle in the Principle of Happiness.

Wisdom—the right knowledge of the Truth

The second principle is "wisdom." As I mentioned before, it is important to have correct knowledge of the Truth. Without correct knowledge of the Truth, human beings cannot be free in the truest sense. I myself feel truly free because I am confident that I know many things.

Take, for example, Christian missionaries who come to Japan. They try hard to convert people to save them, and they say, "Throw away your Buddhist altar and convert to Christianity. You cannot enter heaven unless you abandon Buddhism." They may be pure in heart and devoted but, unfortunately, they are unaware of the Truth. They believe that unless people abandon their faith in "heretical" Buddhism, they cannot go to heaven, and they feel relieved to see people converting to Christianity and say, "Now you can go to heaven." High spirits in heaven feel sad when they see this. Jesus has been ashamed of this for 2,000 years. Many Christians believe that only Christianity can save people because they do not know that Truth can also be found in other religions. They are doing this out of their faith in Jesus, but Jesus himself feels regret about this toward other spirits. He thinks, "There is Truth in Buddhism and Shinto, too. But because I did not teach this, they are saying such things." It is very sad.

So I would like you to have the correct knowledge of the Truth. This is the real meaning of the phrase, "The Truth will set you free."

Self-reflection—correcting your mistakes

The third principle is "self-reflection." This is closely related to the exploration of the Right Mind. We are essentially all children of God with brilliantly shining souls. However, just as a diamond accumulates dirt if it is left untouched, our souls inevitably collect dust and grime as we live in this world. This diamond has to be polished, and this is our spiritual discipline.

Of course, there may be help from an outside power; it is like getting help from a diamond polishing specialist. And sometimes we need such help. But instead of simply doing nothing and waiting for help, we need to polish our own diamond. If we do not refine it ourselves, what is the meaning of spiritual discipline in this world? For what reason do we each have a unique character? Having different personalities means each of us is expected to grow while valuing our individuality.

If you realize you have made a mistake, who can correct it other than yourself? Although someone else could wash your physical body, only you can cleanse your soul; you are responsible for polishing it. Self-reflection is based on the power of the self, which is very important. Please start by reflecting on your past thoughts and deeds. It is no use plating metal before removing rust. If there is rust beneath it, the shiny surface will soon peel away.

The monism of Light is Truth, and it is a teaching of tathagatas. But there is no tathagata among you in this world. No one has attained the enlightenment of a tathagata. One can become a tathagata in a single leap if he or she is a step away from becoming a tathagata, but no one is at that level.

The teaching of self-reflection is the path to the level of arhat, the upper realm of the sixth dimension. Arhat is the preparatory stage for becoming an angel or a bodhisattva. Before entering this gateway to the level of bodhisattva, it is essential to follow the path of self-reflection. To achieve the level of arhat, you must endeavor to remove the "rust" from your mind, allowing a spiritual aura or halo to emanate from you.

Some people say it is hard to become a member of Happy Science because only one-third of the people who sign up are admitted (at the time of this lecture), but this is quite lenient compared to Shakyamuni Buddha's order. In those times, people were not admitted into the order unless they practiced self-reflection in the woods for a week and emitted a halo. If I made this the condition to join our group, our members would have to take back their membership registration, return their *The True Words Spoken By Buddha* sutra, and spend time in the woods until they are ready. But in today's world, if I say you have to reflect for a week and emit a halo, other religious leaders would be furious. They would say, "How can you gather members like that?"

So, I would like all of you to aim first for the level of arhat; everyone can reach this level in this lifetime. Although everyone has accumulated different karma through past incarnations and everyone is going through different stages of spiritual development, everyone, without exception, can attain the level of arhat. It is much harder to advance to the stages beyond this, but through spiritual refinement, you will certainly be able to develop a spiritual aura and become an arhat. This is why there is something called self-reflection.

Above all, I want to produce 1,000 arhats because 1,000 arhats can change a whole nation. When they work as politicians, teachers, and business leaders, they will exert great influence on the people around them, and society will eventually change. An arhat can influence 50 or even 100 people, so if there are 1,000 arhats, about 100,000 people will gradually change. I believe this is the right way to spread the Truth.

Progress—developing the self, others, and society and building utopia

Self-reflection precedes the fourth principle, "progress." If people seek progress without the practice of self-reflection, some will most likely stumble. It would be like plating metal before removing the rust. It would be in vain because you cannot plate metal with gold if the surface is rusted. So first, aim to attain the level of arhat, and then take a great leap to tathagata.

The monism of Light is the teaching of tathagatas if it is taught correctly. To become a tathagata or a child of God who embodies His light, you should first aim to achieve the level of arhat. Only when you have become an arhat and attained a certain level of enlightenment can you advance to the level of bodhisattva. Bodhisattva is a stage at which you save people, but before saving others you need to become aware of your true nature, to some extent. Those who have succeeded in saving themselves are called arhats, and through the practice of loving others and helping others, arhats become bodhisattvas. Bodhisattvas then proceed to the Tathagata Realm, where there is no darkness, no evil, and no shadow—only light.

On seeing these steps, you will understand that the dualism of good and evil does not conflict with the idea that only light exists (except when "light only" is taught as the laws of *tengu* [long-nosed goblins]). It is a matter of the different stages. Eighty percent of people first need to practice self-reflection in the world of duality, and those who have finished cleaning their souls can then enter the level of tathagata. This is an undeniable fact because there are distinct levels in the spirit world (although the eighth dimension is the world of tathagatas, the fact that hell exists cannot be denied).

The spirits in the fourth dimension cannot leap straight to the eighth dimension; they first need to move up to the fifth dimension. The spirits in the fifth dimension must first aim to go to the sixth dimension, then to the Bodhisattva Realm of the seventh, and then to the Tathagata Realm of the eighth dimension. You cannot suddenly skip over the dimensions. As such, progress comes after self-reflection.

I would like all of you to experience progress because without the feeling of making progress, you cannot truly be happy. The last principle in the Principle of Happiness is progress, the development of the self and then of others and society. The ultimate goal is to build Buddha Land utopia. I would like you to follow this path.

The four principles in the Principle of Happiness are love, wisdom, self-reflection, and progress. These are the modern Fourfold Path that will lead you to true happiness. I would like all of you to start along this path. This is the first gateway to the Hinayana path that I teach. Later on, there will be further steps, but at this stage, I would like you to explore the Fourfold Path of love, wisdom, self-reflection, and progress. You will feel the true happiness that you have never felt before. I'm sure about that.

CHAPTER TWO

The Principle of Love

The Second Public Lecture of 1987

Originally recorded in Japanese on May 31, 1987
at Chiyoda Ward Public Hall in Tokyo, Japan
and later translated into English.

1

The Laws of the Sun
through the Passage of Time

Originally, while I was preparing for this second lecture on May 31, 1987, I did not know if *The Laws of the Sun*, my first theoretical book based on my thoughts, would be ready in time for this lecture. So I asked the publishing company to make sure that the printed copies will be ready. This is because more and more people who read over ten of my spiritual message books want to know what my teachings are. So, I thought now is the time that I convey my own thoughts. *The Laws of the Sun* is my first theoretical book, and many of you who have read it must have felt how extraordinary it is. This is, however, only the beginning of the Truth that I will be teaching. From now on, you will be seeing a very grand and extensive Truth being taught in front of you. Today's lecture is also an event to commemorate the publication of *The Laws of the Sun*, so I will start by talking a little about the book.

Fifteen thousand years ago today, the island (Java Island, Indonesia)—in which the city Jakarta now lies—located directly south of Japan was at the center of an enormous continent. The continent was called Mu, and there a country, known as the Mu Empire, flourished. This large continent, however, sank into the ocean about 15,000 years ago. Some of you may have read or heard about this continent in theosophy books or various books outside of our publications.

On that continent, a great emperor was born about 16,000 years ago today. His name was Ra Mu, meaning "the Light of Mu." "Ra" means "light" (sometimes used to mean "king"), and "Mu" was the name of the empire. Ra Mu lived until he was 73 years old, and during his time, the Mu Empire enjoyed the last of its prosperity. What Ra Mu taught at the time was the Laws of the Sun, and *The Laws of the Sun* is very similar to what Ra Mu taught the people of the Mu Empire about 16,000 years ago.

Later, the life of Ra Mu incarnated in the Atlantis Empire a little over 12,000 years ago today. Where now lies the Atlantic Ocean that connects Europe and North America, there was an area called the Bermuda Sea, and a great empire lay there at the time. The Atlantis Empire was highly advanced in scientific technology, and in some ways, the level of its technology surpassed that of today's level. Of course, they were behind in some areas, but in other areas, they were ahead.

For example, the Atlanteans used to travel by air, as they already had airships. I've mentioned this briefly in *The Laws of the Sun*, but the airships were whale-shaped and were 20-30 meters (66-98 feet) long. On top of the airships were small pyramids that looked like dorsal fins. They converted solar energy into power to turn the tail propellers. The upper part contained gas that kept the ship afloat, and underneath it was space for a few dozen passengers. They were powered by solar energy, so they could not fly on cloudy or rainy days. They also had ocean transport that used solar power. They were like present-day submarines, shaped like orcas. In place of where the dorsal fin would be on these submarines, there were three pyramids. These submarines, which also operated on solar energy, had to sometimes surface to absorb sunlight and recharge their battery-like apparatus before submerging again. In terms of how the nation was run, Atlantis already had an early form of democracy that we have today. In this way, this empire was highly developed.

Here, on this land, a part of Ra Mu's life incarnated as Thoth about 12,000 years ago. Thoth was a scientist, politician, and religious leader. The major politicians back then could work in different fields, including religion and science, at the same time. What Thoth mainly taught, in terms of *The Laws of the Sun*, was the principle of love and the structure of the universe, which is essentially the principle of wisdom.

The life of Thoth then incarnated once again, about 7,000 years ago today. This time he was born as Rient Arl Croud in the ranges of Andes Mountains that run through Peru, South America. This incarnation was also a part of Ra Mu's life. What Rient Arl Croud taught at the time was how people can discover their original state of mind.

When you go on a helicopter and take aerial shots along the mountains of South America, there you will see strange geometric patterns. You may have seen it on television. The patterns can only be seen from the sky, and they look like runways or, rather, some kind of message. They are shaped like a human figure with its right arm out or its arm uplifted. So why did people back then make such patterns? They did so because they knew that somebody was watching from the sky above. Then, who was looking down at the runways from the sky above? They were not earthly beings. They were the many space beings who had come to Earth from the universe on spaceships. The people of the Inca Empire in the age of Rient Arl Croud regarded them as gods and worshipped them. However, Rient Arl Croud admonished the people, saying, "They are only space beings. They are more scientifically advanced than us, but we, in the past civilizations, have had more advanced technology, so it is hasty to regard them as gods just because of their technological achievements." Then he taught, "God is not something that exists outside of you; God is within you. God is in yourself. Try and discover God within yourself, not in space beings." At the time, people's minds were facing outward, but Rient Arl Croud turned them inward.

Later, the life of Rient Arl Croud was born in Greece about 4,200 years ago, this time under the name Hermes. Many people today are familiar with the name. Hermes is known as the god of music, but music was merely a hobby that Hermes enjoyed; it wasn't the core of what he taught people. Hermes lived about 500 years before Zeus's birth in Greece, to set the stage. What he mainly taught was prosperity, and this teaching continues to be passed down as the Laws of Prosperity. This prosperity corresponds to the principle of progress that I now teach. The teachings of progress and prosperity were already taught in Greece about 4,200 years ago. As these teachings of prosperity spread, arts and literature flourished throughout the country. This was how Greece became very rich in arts and became the foundation for Zeus to be born and become active as a god of art.

This life of Hermes is a part of an enormous life, and a different part of this life was born again in India about 2,600 years ago. This life is the well-known Gautama Siddhartha, Shakyamuni Buddha. Hermes mainly taught about progress and prosperity, and consequently, the Greeks enjoyed wealth and peace while this Truth was practiced correctly. But as people began to misinterpret the teachings, they became corrupt and strayed to decadence from prosperity. Watching this from heaven, the life of Hermes decided to teach people the opposite of progress and prosperity in his next incarnation—in other words, to be born as Gautama Siddhartha and mainly teach about emancipation and how to abandon worldly attachment. In India, he taught, "True happiness is not found in trying to achieve worldly desires. True happiness can be found when people abandon their attachment. The kingdom of your mind is of great value that no one can invade, even if you have no money, social status, or fame."

Gautama was born a prince and lived in glory until he was 29 years old, but he renounced this life of luxury and set out as a mendicant. For six years he trained in the mountains, meditated, and sought enlightenment with absolutely nothing. He thought, "The fame, status, and luxury that I had for 29 years are what people are eager to have, but they are meaningless. I started with nothing when I was born into this world, and now I will start again from zero. I will start from zero and see how enlightened I can become." This is what the life of Gautama Siddhartha explored. When Gautama was 35 years and 8 months old, he attained the well-known enlightenment beneath a pipal or Bodhi tree. I will reveal his enlightenment and his true thought—what he taught in the 45 years after he became enlightened—in the lecture "Principle of Enlightenment" that I will be giving at Koganei Public Hall on October 10, 1987.

In this way, the life of Ra Mu incarnated as Hermes, who taught prosperity and progress, and as Shakyamuni Buddha, whose teachings were mainly on self-reflection. This was how the Laws of the Sun that Ra Mu taught 16,000 years ago progressed throughout the years. Now, these teachings have been passed on to me. I have talked about the Principle of Happiness in my first public lecture and taught the following four paths as the starting point: love, wisdom, self-reflection, and progress. The teachings of love and progress are essentially the teachings of Hermes, whereas the teachings of wisdom and self-reflection are those of Shakyamuni Buddha. I set these two—"outward teachings" and "inward teachings"—like a pair of wheels when I started this activity. This is the historical background of *The Laws of the Sun*, the first theoretical book that I published.

2

The Prophecy of Salvation

The appearance of *The Laws of the Sun* at the end of the 20th century in Japan was already predicted over 400 years ago in France by Michel de Nostredame (Nostradamus). Some of you may remember the popularity of Nostradamus a while ago. A prophet named Nostradamus wrote the book *Les Prophéties*, which is a collection of poetry of symbolic prophecies. These predictions were not detailed, but he predicted all kinds of incidents that may happen in the future.

His predictions in this book, however, do not go beyond the year 2000. Some of you may know about the significant event that he prophesied would happen in July 1999. He predicted that this event could mark the end of humankind. However, this very difficult book of poems also says, "If the world continues as it is, it may end in the year 2000, but there still is hope." He then explains what this hope is. "Hermes will appear again in the East, and the prosperity of Hermes will save humankind. Also, The Laws of the Sun will be taught in the East, and the descendants of angels who will be born at this time will save the world. This is one possibility. But if this possibility does not come to fruition, the history of humankind will end in the year 2000. Only when The Laws of the Sun will be taught in the East, shall humanity see the creation of a new Golden Age."

I now stand before you to create history beyond the year 2000. In my next theoretical book, *The Golden Laws*, I describe in detail the history of the angels in the West, the East, and Japan. Nostradamus's prophesies may not have gone as far as the year 2000, but *The Golden Laws* will teach you how the future of humanity will unfold. This will be the coming of the Golden Age, and I am not the only one who has spoken about it.

You all who have gathered here today were born to build this Golden Age that will unfold from Japan. You are not here by chance to hear my first or second lecture. You are all here today because you have listened to my voice many times in the past, throughout tens of thousands of years. Just as you hear my words today, you have sat before me and studied my words. Just one or two people are not enough to create the Golden Age; to create the future of humankind for the year 2000 and onward, we must create the first powerful movement from Japan. We were born into this world to turn the first cog of this movement. I predict that many angels born all over Japan will gather to join our movement before the end of this year.

I have not descended to Earth just to establish a single religious group. That is not why I am here. There already are many religious founders who claim to be Messiahs in Japan, so if all I needed to do was start a single religious group, then I would leave it to them. But that is not why I have come. I have come down to unite all the different religions that have originally come from one God and to build the foundation of the Golden Age.

The first phase of Happy Science's movement would be religious reformation. However, my intention is not to destroy or confuse other religious groups or to say, "Only my teachings are right." When a great wave occurs, many things will happen. So as we develop, many whirlpools may form, and the movement may destroy some religions. This is my prediction. A number of religious organizations will collapse and be destroyed as our movement creates a greater surge (later, in 1990, this is what actually happened). However, strictly speaking, this destruction is not just for the sake of destroying them. We are doing a religious reformation to make a great integration, and it is the first part of the process. This movement will start this year (1987), and for the next 10 years, it will reform religions. This religious reformation will spread like wildfire everywhere in Japan.

This is, however, not our ultimate aim. This is only the first stage. In the second stage, our teachings will bring change to the country of Japan as a whole. They will reform everything from its roots, including politics, economics, education, the arts, literature, and the business world. Also, in this second stage, academic studies will be integrated. In other words, when studies are integrated, the modern worldly values that make religion incompatible with politics will be reversed 180 degrees, and what should be at the center will be put back to its original place, as central to all other values.

The question is, what does it mean to govern Japan or this world? As this world is God's creation, those who govern a country must be God's envoys and act on His behalf. So they need more than just political skills or popularity. If the people who govern our society do not know the Truth, how is it possible to create a utopia on earth? It would be impossible.

In this second stage, about 10–20 years later, the Truth will then move beyond the world of religion and philosophy and spread to other fields. For a few years from now, the movement will only influence the world of religion, but later, things will be different. A great shake-up will occur and cause Japan to greatly rebuild its foundation. When it is time, a large number of fighters who help build a utopia, such as those who rose during the Meiji Restoration, will appear. Many of you listening to my lecture today are here to learn the teachings of the mind, but I want you to remember that such fighters will appear in the second stage.

Then this movement will enter the third stage 20–30 years from now. In this stage, our books will have already been translated into many languages and published worldwide, but these books are not merely religious thoughts. They will create a surge for the utopian movement on earth that will spread from Japan to the whole world.

When Shakyamuni Buddha taught the Truth in India, he could only see the whole world from the standpoint of India because of the restrictions of those times. He forecasted that the high-level teachings that he left behind in India would spread to China and Japan someday, but in spite of that, he was not able to leave behind the Truth that is of such a grand scale in his lifetime. Jesus Christ faced a similar situation. Two thousand years ago the king of Israel, Jesus, was born as a Savior to save the world, but unfortunately, the constraints of the times also affected him. Jesus was active mainly in Israel. In the same era, various people in other countries were creating their own cultures and practicing their own political and religious beliefs, so they regarded Jesus's teachings as foreign to their own beliefs. So, even a Savior with a mission to deliver teachings to save the whole world cannot do so if the era is not ready for it.

Now we live in very fortunate circumstances. What I say today will not only be heard by the 900 people who have gathered today. My voice is recorded on tape as I speak, and this recording will spread across Japan and will also be left for the people of the future and spread across the world. We are in such an advantageous situation.

How many people heard Jesus's sermon that he gave with all his might? How many people heard his famous sermon on the Mount? No matter how loudly he spoke, it couldn't have reached more than a thousand or two thousand people. Most people could only get a glimpse of him from a distance. Jesus's teachings are being handed down in the Bible that was put together by his disciples in an incomplete way.

3

Jesus's Teaching on Love and Its Limitations

As you already know, Immanuel or Jesus Christ started his great work after he was baptized at the age of 30 by John the Baptist 2,000 years ago. Soon after he began, twelve apostles gathered around Jesus to help him. They memorized his words and spread his messages to different places.

When Jesus was nearly 33 years old, a young man who was not yet 20 accompanied him. He went wherever Jesus went, taking care of his daily needs such as preparing his food, studying his teachings earnestly, and memorizing them. The young man's name was Mark, and he was the author of the first Gospel in the New Testament. He reincarnated as Advisor Saburo Yoshikawa.

In this way, guiding spirits have descended to earth and taught the Truth throughout different ages, but the most difficult problem in every age has always been about how to spread the Truth. Jesus spoke many beautiful words during his three years of missionary activities; unfortunately, less than one percent of what he said was recorded. The words of Truth that remain in the Bible are only equal to two or three of my lectures. Very few of his teachings were preserved.

Yet I know exactly what discipline Jesus underwent from his birth until the age of 30, as well as his thoughts and his teachings from the age of 30 until he was crucified at the age of 33. I know it all. Why? That is because I, who stand before you now, was one of the guiding spirits who was guiding Jesus at the time. Now he is one of my assisting spirits, so I often communicate with him spiritually. Two thousand years ago, I was the one who communicated with him to suggest ways of conveying the Truth.

Jesus often prayed. Early in the morning, while people were still sleeping, he would go to the Mount of Olives, kneel, and pray to heaven. Among the high spirits who had been sending him messages at the time was Elijah. I mentioned him in the first lecture I gave in 1987, so you may have already heard of the name, but he is a guiding spirit who was born a little over 2,800 years ago. But the being whom Jesus called "My Lord" or "My Abba (Father)" is El Cantare or, in other words, myself.

At the time, I used to mainly talk to Jesus about the different stages of love. As many of you are aware, there are stages of enlightenment in Buddhism. In the same way, love also has stages. Christians today are not familiar with this Truth, but there are stages of love. And because this Truth was not successfully taught in Christianity, it caused Christianity and Buddhism to go separate ways.

To Jesus, I often said, "Love has stages, and human beings need to progress through these stages and become enlightened in this order." But unfortunately, the people who gathered around Jesus were not spiritually mature enough to understand the stages of love. The twelve apostles were no exception. Although they were very close to Jesus, they had difficulties understanding that love has stages as you become enlightened. The reason is that most of his disciples were, for example, poor fishermen who had not studied the Truth well enough. In other words, because the "knowledge" or "wisdom" that we currently teach about was not a part of Christianity's teachings back then, Jesus could not teach them that teachings have stages.

Originally, Jesus had planned to guide people step by step. But the unexpected, or it might have been expected, difficulties more than necessary had arisen to block his way. This difficulty is religious persecution. The persecutors took Jesus's teachings and criticized him by name as a false prophet who teaches false teachings. These leading persecutors were scholars of law. These scholars were specialists in the study of the Ten Commandments that Moses, who led the Exodus more than 3,150 years ago, received at Mount Sinai. They followed Moses's teachings faithfully, focusing on the details of what Moses had said and constantly debating over the interpretation. They would argue back saying, "But Moses said this and that." These people, who lived over a thousand and a few hundred years after Moses, could not understand that Moses was also subject to the constraints of his time. So the Israelites believed that Moses's teachings were perfect and followed what he said: "Let the week be seven days, and observe Sunday as the Sabbath. Rest on the Sabbath day. Do not work on this day."

The truth is, however, the Sabbath is an expression of God's compassion. God commanded human beings to work six days a week. But He did not command to simply rest on the last day of the week. He asked people to use the last day of the week for devotion to Him. He meant that on busy working days, people do not have time to sit quietly, face to face with God, so it is important to set aside one day a week to calm the heart and mind and to make that day a sacred day, a holiday. A holiday was originally a "holy day."

However, upon seeing Jesus's teachings spread like wildfire throughout Palestine, the scholars felt threatened. They thought that unless they took action, their positions as clergies would be jeopardized and that Jesus might deprive them of their jobs. So, just as the Brahmins accused and condemned Shakyamuni in India 500 years before Jesus, they accused and condemned Jesus and demanded his life. They laid traps to snare Jesus at every opportunity.

For instance, they brought a sick man to Jesus on the Sabbath and watched what he would do. Jesus, of course, did not leave the sick man waiting until the next day. When healing people, he always asked, "Do you believe me?" When the sick answered, "Lord, I believe," Jesus would say, "Be as you believe yourself to be." What he meant was, "If you believe that you are a child of God, then rise up as a child of God." The sick rose up. It was not Jesus who had healed him; the man returned to his original state as a child of God by awakening to this Truth. But on witnessing this, the scholar accused Jesus, "You broke God's Commandment and worked on the Sabbath. I saw you healing a sick person." Jesus replied, "Then I will ask you, do you think the Lord God has ever taken a rest for even one day since He divided this universe into heaven and earth? If God rested, even for a day, how can the sun continue to shine? How could all of the creation continue to live? Has the sun ever stopped giving out energy to us, for even a single day? Has the sun ever observed the Sabbath and rested for one day a week? Like the sun, God has never ceased working since the day He divided the universe into heaven and earth. If so, why am I, as a child of God, prohibited to heal a sick person on the Sabbath? Let me ask you this. If a lamb fell into a hole on the Sabbath, will you wait until the next day to rescue it? Surely you will help it right away. It does not matter what day it is to save the eternal life of a human who is closest to God as a child of God. You are mistaken." This is what Jesus said. He spoke the Truth, but his lecture, as shocking as gales or thunder, created many enemies.

At that time, what I said to Jesus was, "Be patient, and teach the Truth step by step. People cannot become enlightened instantly, so do not be hasty. Be patient. You need to start by educating people in steps. O Jesus, Immanuel, should you not, your life will not last for more than three years. Is that what you want?" But Jesus replied, "I would not regret losing my life. I cannot rest, even for a day, even for a moment. When the children of God are suffering so much, what is there to do other than to remove their sufferings? No doctor would leave a patient bleeding with a thorn stuck in his body, and no teacher would watch a student fail and not offer a helping hand." This is how he replied.

Jesus chose to save the lives of many people rather than his own. I thought Jesus should preach for longer and save more and more lives, but he could not wait for long. So he worked hard to save as many people as quickly as he could, and consequently, his impatient character led him to lose his life early. His original plan was to teach several stages of love and lead people to a certain level of enlightenment, but his enemies appeared unexpectedly early, and it became his biggest challenge to resolve conflicts with his persecutors.

Being constantly exposed to danger, his daily life became a severe ordeal, as if walking on thin ice. You may remember his words in the Bible: "Foxes have holes and birds have nests, but the Son of Man has no place to lay his head." Jesus had no place to sleep whereas even birds did. In other words, wherever he went, there would be somebody who were after his life. Day after day he fled, moving from house to house where people hid him.

Jesus could not establish the foundation for his teachings on love, as had been originally planned. He had no choice but to teach mainly of the love that "negates evil within a dualistic way of thinking," as symbolized by his words, "Love your enemies." This is because his disciples were ready to fight his enemies to protect him. For this reason, he said, "Love your enemies and pray for those who try to persecute you. What will you bear by praying for those who love you? Even the other religions do this. If you have studied my teachings, you should pray for the people who persecute you, or try to kill you, not only for the people who support you." Thus, forgiveness became the core of his teachings of love.

So, Jesus taught about love by dividing it into two different types. Forgiving love is the state of mind that arises from attaining the third stage of wisdom, but Jesus taught about practicing forgiveness toward a person.

Then Jesus's teachings of love came to be summarized into two statements: "Love your neighbors" and "Love your Lord Father, Lord God."

He once taught, "To love your family is not so difficult. Look at animals: they cherish their young. If animals can do this, why is it such an effort for you? It is important to love your father and mother, your daughter and son, but as human beings, it is natural to love your own family. Then what is it that is important?" This is why Jesus taught, "Love your neighbor." Then, what did he mean by "neighbor"? It is somebody who you have met in the course of your life. This does not mean your neighbor who you coincidently live next to. Jesus taught people to love others whom we meet in our lives. And the love that you should cherish more is, "Love your Lord God with all your heart, with all your soul, with all your life."

So Jesus emphasized the slogan, "Love your enemies," and also taught people about "love for neighbors" and "love for Lord God"; but unfortunately, his life was cut short before he could teach the next stage. This is why heaven sent Saint Bernard to Europe in the Middle Ages around the 11th century to explain the different stages of love. He was an abbot, one of the famous saints of Europe, who taught that the highest stage of love is to serve your life on behalf of God. However, even Saint Bernard's teachings were not enough. His soul was in reality a reincarnation or a part of the life of Nagarjuna of India, who spread the teachings of Mahayana Buddhism, but he could not explain the stages of love as logically as Buddhism explains enlightenment.

Jesus Christ's teachings of love and Shakyamuni Buddha's teachings of enlightenment come from the same God, so essentially their teachings should not contradict each other. But there is a conflict between the Self-Help sect and the Other-Power sect. While the Self-Help sect acknowledges the stages of enlightenment and encourages self-discipline with faith, the Other-Power sect only emphasizes salvation by faith and loving equally. This is causing conflict between the Self-Help sect and the Other-Power sect. In terms of Buddhism and Christianity, there is a similar issue. Buddhism emphasizes the wisdom of acknowledging differences, but Shakyamuni Buddha originally taught the wisdom of acknowledging equality, too. The latter was later assimilated into Japanese Shintoism, and they said, "All things in the universe, including mountains and rivers, grass and trees, seas and skies, express Buddha-nature or divine nature. Everything has Buddha-nature within." On the other hand, in Christianity, just the wisdom of acknowledging equality is expressed as the teaching of equal love. In short, even though Shakyamuni Buddha had both ideas and taught them properly, Christianity only taught one and could not teach the stages of love from the standpoint of the wisdom of acknowledging differences. So, Buddhists and Christians also find it difficult to mutually understand each other because of their opposing directions.

4

The Developmental Stages of Love

Instinctive love—fourth dimensional love

This is why I have clarified the relationship between the stages of love and the Eightfold Path in *The Laws of the Sun*. Just as there are stages of enlightenment in the Eightfold Path, love has stages.

The love at the lowest stage is the love for family and relatives—the love for parents, for siblings, for a spouse, for children—and men's love for women and women's love for men, or in short, love for the opposite sex. This is certainly one type of love; it occupies 80-90 percent of people's hearts.

Most people think love is something you take, receive, or get from others, but this desire to be loved is not true love. This love is a form of *tanha* in Pali, or thirst, that Shakyamuni Buddha rejected as an attachment. Buddhism sees the word love as synonymous with the word attachment because love for the opposite sex is usually viewed as suffering. Love is regarded as suffering. This love that Buddhism regards as suffering belongs to this stage of "instinctive love," thirst, or *tanha*. Jesus, on the other hand, did not emphasize instinctive love. Although he admitted that instinctive love exists, he focused on the love that is a step higher, "love of your neighbor."

Instinctive love is the fourth dimensional love in the spirit world. If this love goes in the wrong direction in the fourth-dimension Posthumous Realm and it becomes a thirst or an attachment, this can create a realm of hell. In the realm of hell, there is the Hell of Lust where people who have made mistakes in love for the opposite sex go, and there they continue to learn about instinctive love.

On the other hand, those who lived only in the state of instinctive love—whether it is only for the love between men and women or parent and child—but were able to gain peace of mind will go to the Astral Realm in the fourth dimension, which is a part of heaven. In terms of dimensions, instinctive love corresponds to the fourth-dimension Posthumous Realm.

In the least, everyone who has departed earth can return to this dimension, so it should not be the purpose or the final goal of our lives to go back to this realm. The world we are aiming for is the world of enlightenment, which is a higher level.

Fundamental love—fifth dimensional love

What is the next stage above the fourth dimensional love or instinctive love? It is the fifth dimensional love called "fundamental love." Fundamental love is "love that gives." It is higher than the love that wants to receive from others or to be loved by others, as it steps into the stage of giving love. The fifth dimension is called the Goodness Realm, and its inhabitants understand that the essence of love is giving and being kind to others. They know that love does not mean receiving money or presents from those they love. People who have understood this return to the fifth dimension.

This love is the same as the love for your neighbor, which means the love that is more than the love for your family with whom you have had strong bonds since birth. It is the love for the people you meet in the course of your life, at your workplace, at school, or in society. It is important to awaken to this love. This is fundamental love, the love that is a stage higher than instinctive love.

You have surely thought about love many times in your life; everyone has thought about love at least once since birth. However, I would like you to check and see if your understanding of love is only as a thirst for love or if it is "love that gives," where you give kindness and treat people nicely. Your answer is a good indication of what stage your mind is at. Please take time to think about this.

Nurturing love—sixth dimensional love

A stage higher than fundamental love is "nurturing love," which is of the Light Realm of the sixth dimension. Nurturing love is a love that guides people, such as the love of a leader or a teacher. There is a prerequisite condition to bring up other people, bring out the divine nature or Buddha-nature within, and enhance their spiritual development in this world.

What is this prerequisite condition? To practice nurturing love, a person must have exceptional qualities; otherwise, it is impossible. You cannot guide others unless you are independent. This is just as Jesus said in the Bible, "If a blind man leads a blind man, both will fall into a pit." To bring up other people, one must place value on improving oneself and make more effort than an ordinary person. Thus, nurturing love is a leader's love or, in earthly terms, the love practiced by those who have worked hard to reach positions commonly held in high regard, such as executives, teachers, artists, writers, doctors, judges, lawyers, politicians, and bureaucrats.

Although they should be practicing nurturing love and guiding others, these people today seem to be working more for their own reputations, statuses, and positions. How many business executives are working sincerely with their hearts? They should be a guiding light or someone who can lead their employees. A leader should guide their followers and be able to do good work at the same time. This is why both ability and capacity are required.

I have just described instinctive love and fundamental love or, in other words, love for your neighbor. This is a love that arises between you and the people you happen to meet in your daily life. On the other hand, nurturing love is a leader's love; it is the love of those who have studied and worked diligently to assume a position of guiding others, so it is more difficult to practice. If leaders with true ability are guiding others and practicing "love that gives" instead of "love that takes" in this world, they will return to the Light Realm in the sixth dimension.

Forgiving love—seventh dimensional love

Above this is another higher world, the Bodhisattva Realm of the seventh dimension. Bodhisattvas are those who finished establishing themselves in the Light Realm of the sixth dimension, who attained a certain level of enlightenment on their own—in other words, passed the stage of *Hinayana*. They have removed the "rust" from their minds, reached the state of arhat, and have a halo. What is more, with an indomitable resolution, they have taken the courageous first steps toward living a life of selflessness and are living a life dedicated to others. People like this reside in the Bodhisattva Realm of the seventh dimension.

They are not only superior to others in a worldly sense; they have also taken a leap and reached a religious state one stage higher. When people simply just live in this world, it is difficult to live for others and manifest love as vast as an ocean. It is impossible to reach this state with worldly education and by acquiring the thoughts and habits of this world only. To reach this state, a spiritual awakening or an encounter with a master is essential. This experience is what helps us attain a religious state of mind and develop a generous mind. In addition, the strict self-discipline that we undergo to build the self is what enables us to be kind to others who have not yet reached the same stage in the truest sense. Only when you have reached this stage can you show true kindness to others and then truly start forgiving others.

You may think it is not so difficult to practice "love that gives." At Happy Science, there are many people with high social status—for instance, professors at universities, doctors, and business executives—that have become our members. If these people work hard, it will not take them long to reach the stage of nurturing love. However, even such people may find it difficult to forgive people who stand in their way, as Jesus taught. It is easy for them to love and guide employees who accept their ideas, but they may feel resentment toward employees who disagree with them; and it is only natural that they may want to punish or demote them. Anyone would naturally just want to help and lead people who accept your ideas as they are. So, how you treat those who oppose you is a test of whether you can make the leap from nurturing love to forgiving love.

Forgiving others is a stage at which the evil of others begins to appear small. As long as you view others as powerful enemies opposing you, you cannot forgive them. But when you develop a heart that is big enough to embrace others, you will jump to a higher religious stage and embody light. You will be able to view those who are lost in this world with kindness, in the same way that Shakyamuni Buddha views people, with compassion. You will gradually attain such abilities.

The state of mind of the bodhisattva is therefore the stage where you can forgive others. As long as you regard someone as equally powerful or stronger than you, you cannot forgive that person. You also cannot forgive a person who is stronger than you. To say that you forgive such a person is merely sour grapes. The state of being able to truly forgive others also means that you have made considerable spiritual progress.

However, this is not the final stage; there is an even higher stage than the forgiving love that Jesus taught. In the stage of forgiving love, one will try to forgive another from a position of superiority, which is still within the realm of normal human behavior. A religious leader may sometimes face abuse from others in which he may try to forgive them by telling himself, "They are abusing me because they simply do not know the Truth." At this very moment, however, he sees himself as superior to others. He is forgiving others because he thinks that he is higher up than other people.

The prerequisite for forgiving love is that one must be more spiritually advanced than others, but this very requirement is a limitation in itself. At the back of his mind, he is thinking, "I can forgive people because I am superior to other people." To think, "Many people criticize me because they have not yet awakened to the Truth. They lack understanding. But because I understand the Truth, I will forgive them," is a very generous way of thinking that embraces others, but such a person still sees himself or herself as greater than other people and still has much further to go. Above this is the love of the tathagata, the love that corresponds to the eighth dimension.

Love incarnate—eighth dimensional love

The love of tathagata expresses the light of God or Buddha; it is no longer a love expressed between human beings. If a person who has attained this stage is living in the same age as you, his or her very existence is a manifestation of love for all humanity living in your age. This is the love embodied by the great figures whose names have been remembered throughout history.

Looking back at human history, there have been extraordinary people. Confucius, for example, was a great figure whose influence extended over 2,500 years of Chinese history. In Greece, the great philosopher Socrates influenced 2,400 years of history. Jesus Christ delivered the teachings of love in Palestine. In recent years, too, many great figures have brought light to the world. For example, Albert Schweitzer was such a person, and Thomas Edison made a difference in the world with science and technology. The very existence of these great figures, and for them to be living in our time, is an expression of love for all humanity.

Their state of mind is higher than the stage of forgiving love, at which people think, "I will forgive him; I know that he criticizes me because he doesn't have much knowledge of the Truth." It is greater. The very being of such a person radiates boundless love in all directions and is no longer a one-to-one love but a love for many, a love for everyone. The person's existence itself is love.

So, I would like you to go through the stages of "instinctive love," "fundamental love," "nurturing love," and "forgiving love" and aim for "love incarnate" and have such greatness that your very existence is a blessing to all humankind. With this love, you are not living merely as a human being but as a manifestation of light. Aim to embody this love, the love of those who come into this world as tools or servants of God to usher in a new epoch.

The goal of your spiritual training is not to reach the first stage of instinctive love but to progress through the four Developmental Stages of Love: through fundamental love, nurturing love, and forgiving love to love incarnate.

Love of the Savior—ninth dimensional love

Even higher is the stage of "love of the Savior" of the ninth dimension or the world of the Savior. This love is even greater and is beyond the reach of people on earth. Many religious founders of new religions today attempt to preach the love of the Savior, but this results in the misleading of people. You need to know that before teaching about the love of the Savior, you must fulfill each stage of instinctive love, fundamental love, nurturing love, forgiving love, and love incarnate. Without having fulfilled each of them, many religious founders have tried to teach the Truth like a Savior and are deluding people. So please remember these stages.

I have described love in relation to the stages of enlightenment. I hope that you will, using these four stages of love as guidelines for your spiritual training, continue to study the Truth.

CHAPTER THREE

The Principle of
the Mind

⬩⬩⬩⬩⬩⬩⬩⬩⬩⬩⬩⬩⬩⬩⬩⬩⬩⬩⬩

The Third Public Lecture of 1987

Originally recorded in Japanese on July 26, 1987
at Koganei Public Hall in Tokyo, Japan
and later translated into English.

1

Starting from the Teachings of the Mind

Before giving this lecture, "The Principle of the Mind," I published *The Golden Laws*, which is a book on history or time. *The Laws of the Sun*, a commemoration of the second lecture "The Principle of Love" that I gave on May 31, is my basic book of the Truth. Whereas *The Laws of the Sun* is a mixture of the "enlightenment of the individual" and the "enlightenment of the whole," *The Golden Laws* is a book that reveals the history of the light of angels.

Why did I publish such a book now? I wanted to clearly show you the historical meaning of the teachings I am giving you right now. I did not come to earth just to add a new religion to the countless religions that already exist in Japan. Our mission is written in *The Golden Laws*. It is to gather, at the end of the 20th century, all the past civilizations and cultures that have progressed and prospered in many forms, reassess them all, and pave the way for humanity in creating history for the 21st century and beyond. So the Laws I will be teaching from now on will be in light of such an enormous foundation. Please understand this.

As we have repeatedly mentioned, the motto of Happy Science is, "First strengthen the inside and then the outside" or "Build the foundations and then the pillars." That is because a castle built on sand will soon collapse, no matter how grand its appearance. This is true for individuals as well as our organization Happy Science and the structures of the teachings. Without building a firm foundation, it is impossible to build great things. I have already published 20 books (as of July 1987) before giving this third lecture this year. However, 20 books are not enough to cover the foundation of our teachings; we need more. We are scheduled to publish over 20 more books by the end of the year, and you shall begin to see the foundation or framework of our teachings within them.

Many believers and lecturers of other religious groups have become members of Happy Science. We are a very tolerant organization on the whole, so regardless of occupation or position, we welcome anyone who wants to learn our teachings. For example, some believers of Seicho-no-Ie joined Happy Science thinking that their concept of "All religions return to One God" is in line with our teachings. But over time, the difference became clearer to them. The difference is that the concept of Seicho-no-Ie's founder is just one part of the overall teachings of Happy Science. Happy Science not only shows you 5,000 years of history, as written in *The Golden Laws*, but also takes into account the history of the creation of the human race, the birth of our planet

Earth, and even the history of human beings before they came to live on Earth.

But before you learn such magnificent Laws that are of a grand structure and become absorbed in its vastness, you should look within yourselves and check your minds. This is what I want to tell you now. Unless you establish yourselves and understand your minds first, no matter how much you learn about human history or the great figures of the past, or even about prehistory, you will never be able to make progress with knowledge alone.

In my first public lecture on March 8, 1987, titled "The Principle of Happiness," I introduced the four basic principles of happiness—love, wisdom, self-reflection, and progress. And in May of the same year, I gave my second lecture on the first principle, the principle of love. Based on this pattern, today's lecture should have been on the second principle, the principle of wisdom. However, this principle is infinitely expansive. No matter how much knowledge you acquire, if you simply become absorbed in accumulating the vast knowledge of the Laws, you cannot expect to make any spiritual progress. So please remember that "Exploring the Right Mind is a prerequisite for acquiring vast knowledge." That is why, at Happy Science, we teach the exploration of the Right Mind before the four principles of love, wisdom, self-reflection, and progress. The exploration of the Right Mind is most important.

You may go without learning about human history or the teachings of great figures of the past, but you must understand what the Right Mind is; for this, "enlightenment of individuals" is the starting point. Just like what Shakyamuni Buddha taught, the enlightenment of individuals comes before the enlightenment of the whole. When people diligently strive to refine their minds and reach a point where they go beyond themselves, only then will they see beyond the self for the first time. It shifts from the self to others, from others to the world, and from the visible world to the unseen world.

In the third chapter of *The Golden Laws*, titled "Eternal Mountains and Rivers," I give a brief outline of Shakyamuni's teachings of Buddhism. Shakyamuni's teachings focused on the idea that "benefiting the self, benefits others," which taught people to refine the self and do good for other people along the way ("self-benefit" here means to refine and train oneself and not ego or self-perseverance). It means we all are responsible for the way we live and the results brought about by the way we live.

The "happiness of the individual" is not dependent on the "happiness of the general." Each of you should first look within yourselves and confidently take responsibility for your thoughts and actions and for the results they bring. Otherwise, how can we bring happiness to others? Please check whether you are trying to flick the fly off of another person's head instead of your own. You should not be going after a fly buzzing above another person's head before you have chased away the fly above your own head.

At Happy Science, I will introduce a grand system of wisdom, but your spiritual discipline must start from learning the teachings of the mind. This should constitute 70–80 percent of your spiritual discipline. Please remember this. No matter how much historical knowledge you acquire, you will not be able to attain enlightenment without this effort. Only by looking within yourselves and attaining enlightenment can you broaden your perspective and develop a great and noble character. You must not forget this process.

2

The Original State of the Mind

What then is the Right Mind? I would like to describe this in further detail. To qualify as a Happy Science member, you must have the willingness to explore the Right Mind every day. What does "Right" here mean? When can you say the mind is "Right"? Is it simply the distinction between right and wrong? Or does it have a deeper meaning? These are the questions we need to answer. The righteousness we expound in our organization is the righteousness that human beings originally had. So our aim in exploring the Right Mind is to restore the mind to its original state—our God-given state from time immemorial.

Although the exact time when souls were created varies from soul to soul, human souls were created roughly several billion years ago. At that time, in a certain place in the galaxy, the great light of God split into light bodies. This was the first historical event that occurred in the creation of humankind. The particles of light, each endowed with individuality, dispersed throughout the universe and began to develop their consciousness and experience their own unique life as time passed.

We need to remember where we originally came from—what kind of thoughts, nature, and ideals we had at the time of our creation. Through my books, I have described the various realms that exist in heaven to let people know about the heavenly world. However, our ultimate goal is not simply to create the ideal world that already exists in the heavenly world on earth. The current state in the heavenly world is not yet perfect. In the heavenly world, the souls of immemorial times were far freer than the souls of today. So, now is a turning point for creating a new history; we must get back the freedom of the soul or the true nature of the soul we had long ago.

What is the essence of the soul? What is the essence of the mind? What was our original state? How are we exploring righteousness to restore this original state? How should it be done? These are the vital points. God is essentially light itself. This light is not like the light of a lamp; it has various attributes such as love, mercy, wisdom, and prosperity. Each of these qualities shines brilliantly like a facet of a diamond. Many spiritual leaders in the world are unable to explain all of the brilliance or the prismatic facets of the diamond. They only focus on one of them. However, it is essential to understand the true nature of the "diamond." By understanding the true nature of the diamond, you will be able to identify the direction of your spiritual discipline.

This diamond is not something that exists outside of you. You may think the other world that extends from the fourth dimension and beyond is an invisible world that exists somewhere far above in the sky. Perhaps you imagine an invisible borderline 500, 1,000, 5,000, or 10,000 meters above you that you will cross to return to the spirit world after you shed your physical body. That is not correct. In truth, every dimension of the spirit world exists within your mind. Sadly, there is not a single person in today's audience of 1,000 people who know of this basic Truth.

3

The Mind, the Soul, the Spirit

Many of you imagine your mind to be like a balloon that fits perfectly inside of your head, and when this balloon loses its shape, you think about fixing it and putting it back into shape again. If you can think this much, then it is true that you are more developed than a normal person. But I dare say to you: the essence of the mind is not a balloon that just sits inside of your head.

When you open your spiritual eyes and gain spiritual sight, you will see that the human mind is like a balloon that is constantly changing shape. I can see every person's mind. But this state of your mind is not your true nature or the real state of your mind. It is just an external manifestation of the real state of your mind that you are spiritually seeing.

If your mind is harmonized, it appears beautifully round, like a full moon or a ball. But if your mind is unbalanced, the ball will be misshapen. For example, the area of emotion may have grown disproportionately large in some people. Others may have an overwhelmingly large intellectual area. If a person has studied the Truth only in an academic way, like a professor, for 30, 40, 50, or 60 years of his or her life, the intellectual area in the mind would be deformed. Furthermore, there is an area of reason. This area makes people levelheaded, but if it is overly developed, it can make them less likely to respond with emotions. This area of reason in the mind would be protruding out. The area of thought energy is another area of the mind. When you see it spiritually, this area is sitting on top of the ball of the mind, and this is where some people create all kinds of emotional thoughts. This thought energy area of the circular ball is where most of the suffering of human beings is created.

It is commonly believed in modern medical science that the mind exists in the cerebral cortex of the brain, but this is not true. Your mind does not exist within the wrinkles of your brain. You do not think with your brain. The brain is like a control center or a computer room for processing things. That is why, when a person damages the brain or the "computer" where all the commands are made, he or she loses control of his or her actions, speech, and ability to judge. But the "broken computer" and the "operator" are different.

Why doesn't the mind exist within the brain, brain tissues, or brain wrinkles? You may still be in doubt. Some religious people think, "The brain and the mind are different. The mind is everything and not the brain. The brain only makes intellectual or knowledge-based judgments." But we are confident the mind is not in the brain, the cerebrum, or the cerebral cortex. This confidence comes from the spiritual messages you are reading.

Anyone who reads them will realize that each spirit has individuality. Also, depending on how you read them, the spirits' ways of thinking may contradict each other, as they each have different opinions. They are different, but in light of the Truth, each of them is reflecting a correct perspective. Their perspective differs. If all these spiritual messages were my thinking, that would make me a person with a very diverse brain. In truth, they are not my thinking. The spirits' thinking and my thinking are different.

You have read almost 20 books and spiritual message books that I have published, and you may have noticed that different people have said different things. When you read Christian-related books, you may have thought they are genuine. Similarly for Shintoism-related books, you may have thought they are true. Regarding Buddhist-related books also, you may have thought, "yes, they are the truth." Eventually, you would gradually be unable to digest everything. It is difficult to choose when many teachings are of the Truth.

However, their thinking does not coincide with my way of thinking. What they say is the same as me at the root, but they are not completely the same. Of course, the spirits use my brain or brain tissues, or my cerebrum, to judge or think, but their opinions are still different from mine. A spirit once said it accurately, "My body has been cremated and is now ashes, but I still have my way of thinking and individuality" and "What I say in this spiritual message is different from Ryuho Okawa's way of thinking." In other words, even if the body is cremated, the individual will still have consciousness. They can continue to think and will retain their individuality. This fact itself proves that the mind is not in the brain. At Happy Science, we are trying to prove this by demonstrating the different characters of spirits through spiritual messages.

Many people may agree to some extent and say, "I understand that the mind is not in the brain. As you say, it's true that when I'm sad, sadness wells up from my chest. When I'm happy, joy wells up from my chest, not from my head. So I imagine that my mind is not in my head and is located somewhere near my heart." If the mind is not in the brain, which works as the control tower of the body, then what is it? From here, I will talk about whether the true nature of the mind is the sphere-shaped ball that I mentioned earlier or if it is something else.

We often use the words "soul," "spirit," and "mind" without thinking carefully about them. At times, these words are used to mean the same thing, and at other times they mean different things. For example, when a newspaper survey in Japan asked the question, "Do you believe in spiritual beings?" there was only about 20 percent of respondents who answered, "Yes," and about 50 percent who answered,

"Spiritual beings may exist. There is a chance that they might." However, when the question was phrased as, "Do you think that the mind exists?" over 99 percent answered, "Yes." This shows that people are very much influenced by a superficial understanding of these words, and they do not know their true form.

The mind is at the core or the center of the soul. If you could physically see the soul and mind, their shapes do not overlap at all. Their spiritual bodies are different. At the center of the soul exists the mind, which, through my spiritual sight, I can see is shaped like a ball that is around 30 centimeters (one foot) in diameter. As for the soul, it is fitted perfectly inside the physical body in the shape of a human body.

Next is "spirit." What, then, is the difference between "soul" and "spirit"? A soul is shaped exactly like a human body, and this is where his or her own identity comes from. Spirit, however, has a much broader meaning than soul.

Now, if we compare the spirit in humans and animals, they are different. The spirits of animals are not very individualized as human spirits are, so depending on the level of consciousness of the animals, their spirits form a collective spirit. For example, a dog spirit that has departed from its physical body would usually remain in its dog shape and continue to live in the other world. A dog whose consciousness has individualized through its incarnations would stay as a separate dog spirit, but a dog whose consciousness has not sufficiently individualized would be absorbed into a collective spirit. In heaven, dozens of animal spirits sometimes form one collective group. Dog spirits that are of similar consciousness would group and form one collective spirit consciousness under one collective concept. When the time comes, a part of the dog spirit will be born on earth, but when they do, their individuality would be lost.

The same is true for plants. Believe it or not, plants also have a soul. When I take a look at the soul of plants through my spiritual sight, I see small beings that are human shape resembling fairies from fairy tales; they have eyes, a nose, and a mouth, so we can converse with them. This is the shape of their soul. They also return to heaven when they leave this world, but in the case of plants, not many are individualized. So they usually live together in groups. On the other hand, big ancient trees that have lived for hundreds of years—like the ones that are usually near shrines—have usually developed strong individual characters. The trees that have been planted for hundreds of years at shrines have watched human history for centuries, so these trees have developed human-like consciousness. So when they return to heaven, they each keep their consciousness and continue to live like a tree with their character. Put simply, this is the Truth about the spirits of animals and plants.

4

The Relationship between the Stage of the Mind and the Spiritual Form

The fourth dimension—
resembling the appearance of humans

Next, I will talk about the spirits of human beings, which is more complicated. As I explained earlier, a soul that is the same size as the physical body fits inside of it, and after leaving this world, most people will still take the form of a human with arms, legs, eyes, nose, and mouth as well as a head. But in time, souls would begin to realize that they don't need such a form.

Souls that have returned to the Posthumous Realm of the fourth dimension in the spirit world still live a similar lifestyle as humans. They feel uncomfortable if they do not take a human form. Many of them even "eat" three meals a day and feel sleepy at night. They still recognize themselves through their human form from when they were alive on earth, so they feel unsettled without it.

The fifth dimension—recognizing that you can exist without human form

The situation changes the higher up you go in the spirit world—the fifth, sixth, seventh, and eighth dimensions. The fifth dimension, or the Goodness Realm, is a world where good-natured people return, so only harmonious people live here. Even in this world, the spirits continue their spiritual discipline in human form for about 90 percent of the time. But they start to consciously experience the ability to move freely to any place they wish through strange experiences, such as no longer needing to walk on the ground or not dying when jumping off a cliff.

These experiences in the fourth dimension can only happen by chance. They can only happen sporadically under the guidance of various spirits who occasionally help them experience the ability to appear wherever they want or meet whomever they wish. But in the fifth dimension, the souls can do this more or less at their own will. Such experiences prompt them to vaguely think, "Maybe I will continue to exist as a consciousness even without human form." This is when souls start to realize that they are spiritual beings. However, the souls in the fifth dimension are still attached to their human form, so they do not feel comfortable if, for example, he or she, who was 163 centimeters tall, is not the same height.

The sixth dimension—transforming your form

Above this is the Light Realm of the sixth dimension, where things are a little different. This realm also has multiple levels of consciousness. To enter this world, souls need a strong belief that the world they live in is God's creation and is governed by the Truth that comes from God. In this sixth dimensional Light Realm, many people are polishing their souls through the study of this Truth. Along the process, they gradually become free from the consciousness they used to have on earth, the physical senses of their physical bodies. They begin using the knowledge of the Truth that they have acquired to test what they have learned.

You may have heard about willpower, but this sixth dimension is where each soul starts to seriously explore this power. The souls that have reached this stage become aware that they are free from the restriction they had from dwelling in a physical body so their power is much greater. They study various kinds of willpower, and angels who take the role of teachers instruct them about the true nature of willpower.

For example, they first experience how to make an image that is in their mind appear in front of them. Consider this glass of water that is on the podium in front of me; the inhabitants of the sixth dimension know that they can create anything (in spiritual form) at will because they are taught how to do it. So by thinking, "I need a glass of water," they can make it appear on the podium just by using their willpower. In the fourth and fifth dimensions, such experiences only happen spontaneously, and the souls do not reach the level to fully recognize that they can do this by thinking strongly. But in this sixth dimensional Light Realm, the souls know that they can make the glass appear just by thinking about it. So once they learn this, they next try to think about making a patterned drinking glass appear. When they succeed in doing so, they then start wondering if they can fill the glass with water, and indeed water appears. When the glass is filled with water, they drink it and find that it tastes the same as the water they used to drink on earth. In this way, they learn that they can produce water and a glass by their willpower.

After some time, maybe decades or hundreds of years, souls will get bored of simply producing water and a drinking glass and begin to wonder if they can make other things. For example, a female who has an interest in clothes may think, "Perhaps this means I can create clothes exactly the way I want them," and become immersed in making clothes. She may imagine a polka dot dress but end up with a striped dress at first. So she will begin by making a plain, white blouse without any patterns and master this before moving on to produce a skirt of her favorite design. Once she succeeds in doing this, she will go back to making polka dot designs, and this time with the intention of making 20 dots.

But perhaps only 17 will come out, and she will try to figure out why. As she continues to practice in this way, she learns that depending on the nature of her thought, she can also create personal belongings with willpower; and she goes on to think about producing items other than clothes, such as necklaces. Those who are advanced in their training can create excellent necklaces, but beginners have problems at first. Like so, the souls of this realm go through such learning.

Once the souls have reached this stage, their next thought will be, "I used to feel uncomfortable when my form in the mirror was different from how I was on earth. But I'm curious if I can change my appearance into another form." They begin to realize they can not only create clothes but also change their appearances. For example, a spirit who was comfortable being of average height would wonder if he or she could grow a little taller. Once they imagine their body to be seven feet tall, their body will grow taller and taller until it reaches that height. Then, the flowers, trees, and houses around them will start to look smaller than before. As they walk around at that height, they soon start to feel strange and scared and return to their previous size. The first experience usually ends like this. But as time passes, they get the hang of it and begin to grow taller and taller. They may even try to lengthen their arms and realize that they grow as expected. A lengthened neck might be scary, but through these experiences, spirits in the sixth dimension come to realize that the human form they used to have on earth is not their true nature.

Because the spirits of the sixth dimension have reached the stage of high spirits, they will be told to not only concentrate on their studies but also guide people on earth. The sixth dimension is a wonderful place, but they cannot stay there for 400 or 500 years. The spirits from higher dimensions tell them, "Here, the sixth dimension is the realm before the Bodhisattva Realm of the seventh dimension. You now need to learn about helping others." Once the spirits get used to life in the sixth dimension, they start getting the urge to help people and are assigned roles as guardian and guiding spirits of people on earth.

Today the terms "guardian spirit" and "guiding spirit" are used in many different ways, so it may be confusing to try and understand the true meaning of these terms. To put it simply, a guardian spirit is a being that is related to you, and a guiding spirit is a spirit that has specialized abilities in a particular field and guides those on earth when necessary. If a general spirit from the fourth or fifth dimension who is living on earth receives guidance from a guiding spirit of the sixth dimension, he or she will be able to make decisions from a higher perspective.

The kind of guidance that spirits of the sixth dimension give to people on earth is, in most cases, guidance for specialists or experts. Through inspiration, they provide, for example, a scholar with the idea for the theme of his or her thesis or a poet an unexpected idea or poetic words while he or she is taking a stroll down the beach. As for an artist, they could inspire them with images for paintings. Such inspirations usually play a big role in creating great works of art. The spirits in the sixth dimension are in charge of such work; they give vocational and professional guidance. After they have gone through a certain level of spiritual development in the other world, they start to guide people on earth.

As guiding spirits, they know their true nature is not human form, so when guiding people on earth, they sometimes choose to take a god-like form. If the person on earth has spiritual sight, rather than appearing before them in a tie and a business suit, they might take a god-like appearance. For example, when they appear before the leaders of orthodox religions, they could take the form of a god. In this way, they can transform themselves freely at will.

As I mentioned in *The Laws of Eternity*, on the rear side of the sixth dimension, there is the realm inhabited by *tengu* (long-nosed goblin) and *sennin* (hermit). The inhabitants in some areas of these realms concentrate on enhancing their transformational ability and supernatural powers, such as practicing transforming themselves into various forms. As they become able to change themselves into something other than human beings, they gradually become aware of their true nature. This is when souls begin to understand that they are actually spirits.

The seventh dimension—recognizing that they are a consciousness that gives to others

As souls move from the fifth dimension to the sixth and then reach the Bodhisattva Realm of the seventh dimension, they have more experiences that convince them that the true nature of spirits is beyond the physical human form. Bodhisattvas dedicate themselves to saving all people through acts of love, so they are very busy. To fulfill their duties, they need to separate their consciousness into different roles.

Their human form gradually begins to feel limiting. It is fine being in a human form while they are in training themselves, but they eventually need to take a form that is easier for them to move around in. Along the way, they notice that they no longer have a human form and have become "will" itself. For example, some bodhisattvas belong to the group of medical spirits, and they help heal people's illnesses. When these bodhisattvas busily concentrate on healing people, one day, they notice that they are no longer in human form. They notice that they are working purely based on their consciousness of wanting to help people through medical treatments. As they grind themselves hard at work for eight hours a day, from eight in the morning until five in the evening, at some point they think, "Just now, I forgot that I was a human. My consciousness alone was doing acts of love," and return to their human form again. On and off, bodhisattvas begin to have these sorts of experiences. This is how they recognize themselves to be spiritual beings.

The eighth dimension—role-centered consciousness

When bodhisattvas develop further in their spiritual discipline and reach the Tathagata Realm of the eighth dimension, they attain an even higher level of consciousness. You may understand the soul and spirit through your worldly understanding, but tathagatas clearly know that the essence of being human is not defined by a physical body and life on earth.

Bodhisattvas still follow a similar kind of lifestyle they had when they were alive on earth and take a human form, but this is different for the spirits of tathagatas. If people living on earth tried to picture the Tathagata Realm, they would imagine trees, mountains, houses, and people, but the inhabitants there think and live differently. They recognize themselves as the embodiment of the Laws.

Rather than existing as individual human beings, they exist as consciousness itself acting out its role.

What is tathagata's consciousness? I have explained in several ways that there are seven colors in the spectrum of God's light. For example, the white light is that of love, and the red light of Moses is of leadership, of those who can guide people. The green light is of nature and harmony, and the purple light of order is of Confucius and Amaterasu-O-Mikami. The spirits of the Tathagata Realm work as pure consciousness, representing these lights. However, when they communicate with people on earth or when they appear before people as spirits, they take on a human form. Also, as written in "The Spiritual Messages from Emmanuel Kant," tathagatas occasionally enjoy the private life of being an individual by reading books or going on walks. They each have their personality, so they sometimes enjoy being an individual. But for most of the day during work, they carry out their activity as pure consciousness. They are developed spirits that have this level of awareness. The eighth dimensional tathagatas more or less do not exist as a soul. They have become a consciousness with a role. Although tathagata may live in a human form occasionally when they want to relive memories from their past, most of the time they are consciousness with a role.

As I mentioned in *The Laws of the Sun*, the enlightenment of tathagatas is expressed by "one is many, many are one."

This is a very philosophical term that Dr. Kitaro Nishida (1870-1945), a modern Japanese philosopher of the Kyoto School, introduced. It means that a tathagata spirit can be one entity yet become five entities or be five entities yet become one. In the same way, they can be ten entities yet be one and one entity yet become fifteen. Tathagatas know how many actions they can take on themselves. In the world of tathagata, spirits are not individual beings like human beings but can split into as many entities as necessary.

Before attaining the tathagata level, they advance through many spiritual levels, experience the fourth and fifth dimensions, and perhaps even hell. Through these experiences, they have learned the true nature of spirits and reached a level of awareness that enables them to fulfill their role purely as a consciousness.

The ninth dimension—the source of Laws

Above this is the ninth dimension. Here each consciousness is even larger. In the Tathagata Realm of the eighth dimension, spirits can split themselves for a particular purpose, but in the ninth dimension, each consciousness can take on many personalities for a multitude of purposes, and the consciousness is a big mainstream. For instance, the consciousness of the ninth dimensional Grand Tathagata can be likened to a dam. There are reservoirs that are named after Jesus Christ, Shakyamuni Buddha, and Moses. Each of them stores a great amount of water that reflects their characteristics. And when necessary, they will release this water into various places. This is the "Source of the Laws."

It may be hard to have a clear image of the spirits of the ninth dimension. As written in *The Spiritual Messages from Confucius*, we, the ninth dimensional spirits are not simply one spirit that consists of one core spirit and five branch spirits. If we wish, we can divide ourselves into millions or billions of entities. Their human awareness has almost faded away, but because they have once lived as human beings, they can manifest a consciousness with a personality, if necessary. Their true nature, however, is like a dam at the source of a great river, and the composition of the stored water differs from dam to dam.

So each of us on earth with an identity and a physical body can be likened to a drop of water that flows from a huge dam down to the mouth of a river. This is the difference between the ninth dimensional Grand Tathagata and the people living on earth. If a Grand Tathagata can be symbolized by a dam, perhaps you can imagine how unhuman the image of God may be.

In this lecture, I started exploring and talking about the shape of the mind, but as you keep on exploring, you will notice that the true nature of the mind is something far greater than what we can imagine. A soul with a human shape progresses to become a consciousness beyond a human form, then grows even bigger as a consciousness until it becomes a role itself. Once it surpasses being a role, it eventually becomes the source of the Laws. As we trace it back to its origin, we can understand the true nature of the mind. This is the Truth about the mind, the soul, and the spirit.

5

The Exploration of the Right Mind

Balancing the mind

Now that we have learned about the multi-dimensional world, the question is, what should we do as beings living on earth? We understand that there are ultimately great consciousnesses like dams and that they are roles themselves. However, at present, we are not consciousnesses who are in heaven; we dwell inside these physical bodies. How can we understand our true nature and make the most out of our everyday lives? We have to find the answer to these questions.

The soul is essentially life energy that can expand infinitely, like opening one's hand, and it can contract to a single point, like closing one's hand. When the soul or the spirit expands, there is an infinite universe, and it can also contract to become as small as a mustard seed. However, it is difficult to recognize your consciousness as something that can become as small as a mustard seed, so it is important that you manage your soul that dwells inside your physical body. To do so, we must first try to govern the mind—the mind that is at the core of the soul.

What are the areas that exist in the mind? There is the area of emotions or sensibility, the area of will, the area of intellect, and the area of reason. So when you reflect on your mind, you must check to see if the areas of the mind are balanced. This is the first point.

Is the area of emotions of your mind overly swollen? Have you been able to emotionally stabilize yourself throughout the day, from morning until night? Do you have difficulty controlling your emotions and have ups and downs? Please check if you are an emotional person or not.

Next, we have the area of will. Will is the determination to actualize your intentions. This attitude is very important, but check to see if your will is not too stubborn and you are open to other people's opinions. Although it is good to have a strong will, check to see that you do not always insist on getting your way or are unable to understand the feelings of others. Having a cast-iron will is not necessarily bad, but are you flexible enough to make changes when necessary?

There is also the area of intellect. True intellect includes spiritual wisdom that is emphasized in Buddhism, and you should develop your intellect to this level. However, if spiritual leaders and priests or monks reflect on this area, a priest may discover that he has been merely interpreting the Bible, and Buddhist monks may realize that they have become masters of reciting the sutra rather than teachers of souls. You must also check if the intellectual area of your mind has not become distorted and swollen.

You need to check the area of reason, too. Reason plays the role of a compass, steering the course of a life in the right direction. But if the area of reason becomes over-developed, people tend to be cold and critical and coolly analyze others and their actions, just like a critic who judges others on how he or she will turn out to be. Those who see people and events using reason alone forget the fact that all human souls are essentially brothers and sisters, the children of God, and we are all one.

In this way, first I would like you to make sure that the areas of emotion, will, intellect, and reason are well-balanced and that together they form a perfectly round ball. Please check this every day, for this is the first step in exploring the Right Mind.

Removing clouds from your "thought tape"

What is the second step in the exploration of the Right Mind? As the first step, I explained that you have to make effort to create a well-balanced mind: to correct the distortions in each area to make it round, like a ball. The next step is to remove any clouds of thought hovering over the mind. There is what is called a "thought tape"—where your all thoughts and actions are recorded—on the top of the "ball." The state of this tape determines whether or not you become happy in the course of your life. Through my books, you have probably learned what are good thoughts and bad thoughts. For instance, kindness, sympathy, tenderness, and love for others are wonderful, good thoughts. On the other hand, complaints, anger, jealousy, and envy are bad. These negative, selfish thoughts and desire for self-preservation will never benefit others or yourself. It will create clouds over the thought tape of the mind, which will then block God's light that is bright like the sun.

No matter how bright the sun is shining, we can easily block out the light. Even when the bright sun is shining, we can block it by simply standing under a roof. The true nature of God's will is said to be the light that illuminates everything in all directions without discrimination. This light is unobstructed life energy that pours out in all directions, but because it is light, it has the physical quality of being able to be blocked. As described in *The Golden Laws*, God's light has both affinity and exclusivity. It has an affinity to anything that corresponds to the qualities dwelling inside it, and it repulses or veers away from anything negative that does not correspond to it. This rule is associated with the thought tape of the mind. It means that you can create a roof by using your thoughts. Why can we create such a roof? It is because just like God whom you originate from, you have the freedom to create. You can create a roof that blocks the sunlight using your thoughts. The light that comes from heaven is God's light or energy, whereas the energy with which you create a roof is also the creative energy that is given to all of God's children. Both energies originate from the same source. Because we are given the freedom to create, we can create all kinds of roofs.

In the course of the 40, 50, or 60 years of our life, we unconsciously create clouds, or roofs of thought, by accumulating negative thoughts. These clouds of thought block God's light. What happens, then, if the light is blocked? No matter how hard your guardian or guiding spirits try to help you correct the course of your life, the clouds over your mind will shut out even their guiding light. It means that you, yourself, chose to live in darkness. Unknowingly, you create clouds in your mind, block out the light, and live in darkness. So the principle of happiness is to remove these clouds of thought by your own efforts because you, yourself, are the one who created the clouds. If your house becomes messy, whose responsibility is it to clean it? Would the town hall send cleaners for you if you were to call them? No, they wouldn't. You must clean the mess you made in your own house. It is as simple as this.

A certain religious group claims that God saves everyone and that suffering that arises in the course of a life is the state of bad karma disappearing. But the cause of suffering is you, yourself. You were the one who created the thought cloud that blocks God's light and makes it difficult to receive the guidance of your guardian and guiding spirits. As a result, you will live under the cloud, lead a wrong life, and fall to hell. Your sufferings do not lie in others or what is outside of you; you are the creator of them. If you created your suffering and you made your room dirty, you must realize that the dirt will not go away unless you remove it yourself. In this case, prayer will not clean your room. It will not. You must not get this wrong. This is not the love of God. Do not misunderstand God's love by interpreting it to mean that you can do whatever you want because all suffering is bound to disappear.

You need to understand from deep within your soul that your suffering is the result of the clouds of your thoughts, and unless these clouds are cleared away, you can never live the right way as a child of God. The mistakes you made through your own decisions must be corrected while you are alive in this world by reflecting on your thoughts and deeds and correcting them. You will never be saved by others; only you can save yourself by making such efforts. This attitude is essential, so please do not misunderstand this point.

I would like to remind you of the two points in the principle of the mind, which is a part of the Principle of Happiness. First, keep the different areas of the mind in balance. Second, make efforts to find any clouds in your thoughts, remove them through self-reflection, and restore your mind to its original state. This is the only way to attain true happiness. Please remember these two points.

CHAPTER FOUR

The Principle of Enlightenment

The Fourth Public Lecture of 1987

Originally recorded in Japanese on October 10, 1987
at Koganei Public Hall in Tokyo, Japan
and later translated into English.

1

The Passion to Seek the Truth

A year has already passed since we established Happy Science on October 6, 1986. In that time, this movement has grown so rapidly—faster than what I as the President (currently, Master and CEO of Happy Science Group) expected. To start off, I limited the number of new members, but day by day, more and more people started to apply for admission. I based the admission on an application form, which included an essay explaining their purpose and aspirations for joining (at the time of the lecture). But as days went by, the number of applications was more than what I could read. We were working quietly because I wished to carry out our activities discreetly for the first two or three years. Even so, Happy Science currently receives over 3,000–5,000 letters from people every month. I read the letters, as I want to know people's thoughts, but unfortunately, the number of them has been too many to reply to since April 1987.

When thinking about the development of this movement in two years', or even three, five, 10, or 20 years' time, we need to establish a strong and firm foundation based on a clear vision. This is because there is a high risk of us losing control because our momentum and energy are so great. So I courageously decided to take a firm stance. As those of you who have become our members may have noticed, Happy Science is a demanding organization. And as a result, the level of our organization has become very high. Our policy states that as a prerequisite condition, anyone who wants to join is required to have read over 10 of my books. Reading the applications of the new members (at the time of the lecture), to my surprise, I found that every single person has already read over 20 books. The passion of those who have read over 20 books and have written an essay for membership is impressive. We tried to control the number of memberships, but people are doing everything in their power to become a member. This enthusiasm is very impressive. The amount of effort that people make once they become members is also great. Happy Science held a May Seminar, then a basic-level seminar in August, followed by an intermediate-level seminar in September. Since May, I have been writing commentaries on the Truth essays that the members wrote by reading them one by one. What I noticed was how fast they were advancing. They have extraordinary passion. It was amazing. If I had been more generous with marking the essays, everyone would have passed. That's how great their enthusiasm was.

I've already reminded our members many times about the reason I introduced such an examination system; it is so that Happy Science can create a basic framework of our activities from the early stages. Now, our philosophy is to establish a role model of how Happy Science should carry out its activities while we have 1,000, 2,000, or 3,000 members and to run the organization as steadily as possible until such a model is created. Once our membership reaches tens of thousands, it would be impossible for me to nurture people directly; so I aim to raise the level of our current members so that each of them can be a leader to guide the newcomers.

2

Establishing a New System of Values

In terms of whether Happy Science is a religious organization or not, legally, this has not been decided yet; but I say we are an organization with religious aspects (in 1991, Happy Science was officially certified as a religious organization). We rarely see other religious organizations that adopt an examination system. Some may have exams for executives but not for general members. So why does Happy Science hold these kinds of examinations? Even our members have a mixed level of understanding on this.

Here are my thoughts. The pass mark for the basic-level seminar is set at 70 points. At Happy Science, the basic level is equivalent to the enlightenment that enables you to enter the fifth dimension from the fourth dimension. It means people who pass the basic level course have the enlightenment of the fifth dimension or the Goodness Realm. How about the pass mark for the intermediate level? The pass mark is 80 points, and we determine that anyone who passes the intermediate level has the entry-level enlightenment of the sixth dimension or the Light Realm. This is where we set the next level. As for the advanced-level seminar, people who are past this level have reached the state of an arhat. This is the standard measurement I set as indications. This is still the first attempt, so there is space for trial and error; but from what I've seen so far, these stages of enlightenment are more than 80 percent accurate.

We receive all kinds of answers, but we grade and rank them in a certain order. Based on the rankings, we can see a clear correlation 70-80 percent of the time. Those who achieve top grades are usually the same kind of people 70 percent of the time. As for the rest of the people, their rankings do not differ much from their past exams. These are scores, but I would like you to consider what they indicate. I am thinking about them, too. What they indicate are the members' strong yearning to master the Laws and their aspirations to attain enlightenment. It is very clear.

Those who achieve top grades are not necessarily intelligent people. The results show us that the scores are completely unrelated to worldly intelligence, education, status, income, age, and gender. There is no connection, but people who appear disorganized at first can show a certain level of ability. What can this mean? Due to the demanding style that we have adopted, we appear to have gained the trust of much of society. For example, from the end of August to September 10, 1987, five professors from national universities became our members. The addresses they provided in their application forms were of their office, which means that they did not hide their profession. That is how much trust we have gained. Aside from them, many of our members include doctors and presidents of companies. There are many high government officials, too. Many such people have become our members. These people are very intelligent in a worldly sense. The doctors are graduates of the medical faculty of national universities, so they are very intelligent. You may naturally expect these people to achieve high scores on our seminar tests, but this is not the case. It is difficult for them to achieve higher scores. On the other hand, middle-aged housewives or graduates who just finished college often achieve high scores. It is difficult for highly educated people to understand how this could be. They think, "Why can't I get a high score when I am an intelligent person?"

These kinds of questions arise because we are now attempting to establish new value criteria. You may think the current criteria that are accepted in this world are a matter of course. However, these earthly criteria do not always reflect the criteria of the other world. If you liken the value system in the other world to a pyramid, the pyramid in this world would often be inverted or upside down. People who are living and doing absolutely nothing of value in God's eyes are, in some cases, the most highly respected in this world. Most people on earth do not understand what is of true value and what is not. For instance, they think it is important to become famous or to appear on television, whereas others place a high value on marketing themselves or working for a blue-chip company with a good reputation. However, whether you work for a prestigious or mediocre company, there is no correlation between them in regards to which realm in the other world you return to. There is absolutely none. It is in fact sometimes the reverse; people who work for a mediocre company may return to a higher realm than those who work for a prestigious company.

Jesus once taught, "Unless you become like children, you cannot enter heaven." Even so, some people who took our seminar tests cannot believe that young people are getting top scores. They tend to think, "I have been seeking enlightenment through many different religions for decades, so there is no way young people are more enlightened than me." But entering heaven is not dependent on age. People who have accumulated many experiences will not necessarily go to a higher realm in heaven than someone young and inexperienced.

Gender does not necessarily matter when it comes to enlightenment. A husband who acts arrogant does not necessarily return to a higher realm while his wife goes to a lower realm. This is not the case. It is often the reverse. Take for example a husband who was an executive of a prestigious company and a wife who has been a housewife for over 30 years. After they return to the other world, the wife may return to the Light Realm while the husband goes to either hell or the Astral Realm. This is often the case. But people in this world do not understand this. In this way, gender, status, or education does not matter at all. This is the value standard in the real world.

The standard of value has been long taught by various leaders from various angles and ways, but it has yet to be taught in a unified way. Right now, I live in this world with a physical body. But when I am not, the work I do in the heavenly world is to essentially establish a value standard based on the Laws. This is what I mainly do. In this world, there are many kinds of people; a person who studies religion, such as Buddhism, Christianity, or Shintoism, or others who have completely different jobs, such as management executives, scholars, businessmen, farmers, and fishermen. Various people live their lives thinking various thoughts and doing various things. But no matter what kind of lives people lead, their lives will always be measured against a standard in the eyes of God. So then what is this value criterion? What is the mindset of a bodhisattva? What mindset makes a person suitable for the Light Realm? How can it be measured without considering the person's occupation, gender, and age? This is, in fact, my real job. My real job is to make this judgment. For a long time, this is what I have been doing in the heavenly world. I now live in a physical body on earth, but the reason I am living with you all on this earth now is to demonstrate the true values seen from the eyes of God to people in this late 20th century. This is one of my main jobs. I am now attempting to cast light on what has been put under the shadows. This is my job.

You all work in different places, such as companies or government offices. Although you may think that studying the Truth is wonderful, perhaps you still have difficulty speaking about it openly in your workplace. You may feel it would be disadvantageous for you to reveal your interest in spirituality and are considering the pros and cons. But why would you instinctively think in such ways? Why should you weigh things like this? I sometimes receive letters from young women. They all believe in the Truth and wish to keep studying throughout their lives, but their common concern is that they cannot be open about it to their partners before marriage. The women worry that their partners will be surprised upon finding out about their interest in the Truth once married and that their values will be misaligned. Even men who strongly wish to walk a religious life worry that this will become an obstacle when they try to get married. They worry that such a way of life that appears strange to others would work against them if revealed. At workplaces, people on track for promotion often worry about rumors that they are into something strange. For example, some of you may have been invited to play golf on the day of my lecture. You may have turned down the invite and have come here instead. But ask yourself if you could have openly told your colleagues about your plans to attend a Happy Science lecture. I am sure you couldn't. Why? That is because you want to protect yourself from anything that can stop you from getting a promotion.

However, this is not how it should be. You should not be afraid to tell other people about doing the most valuable thing in this world. It means that the value upheld in society is mistaken. If the value is mistaken, all you need to do is change the value. You must reverse the value. We have stood up to show you the new value standard and demonstrate the fragility of the common sense of this world. The time for us has come to show people what real value is and what kind of people are truly great.

3

Enlightenment Starts with Knowing

On passing over to the other world, those who hold themselves in high regard in this world will keenly realize how little their existence is. No matter how big their executive desk might have been, they will come to realize how small they are in the presence of the light of great guiding spirits. At the foot of angels, they will feel so humbled that they will soon start reflecting on themselves. Upon just seeing such great light, they will start to repent. This is a world beyond words.

This happens because they did not know the Truth. However, the responsibility for their ignorance of the Truth lies with themselves. They alone are responsible. So they cannot make any excuses for not knowing the Truth, no matter how little they become when they return to the other world. Opportunities and clues to achieve enlightenment were all around them while they were living on earth. Who mocked those chances? Who scoffed at those opportunities, saying the clues were complete nonsense? People will thoroughly be made aware of their mistakes. Enlightenment starts with "knowing." There is no excuse for not knowing.

The next question is: "What do we have to know?" You must know God, God's will, and the teachings that flow from God's will. Without this understanding, you will not be able to grasp any clues to enlightenment. There are many ways to attain enlightenment, but you can never become enlightened by simply walking in the mountains or sitting beneath a waterfall. The path that leads to enlightenment is the path that leads to spiritual awareness. To attain spiritual awareness, you have to know what is beyond this world. When you have experienced the total reversal of your worldly values, you can be said to have taken the first step toward enlightenment. How can you reverse your worldly values? You can experience this through encountering the Truth. "Knowing" means to first get in contact with the Truth.

The way to come in contact with the Truth is to read books of Truth or listen to my lectures. The book *The Laws of Eternity* is my 24th publication. I published many books in rapid succession. Why did I publish them so quickly? These books are in fact "bullets of light" shot from God. We are shooting these bullets one after another. To convert the value system of this world, we must give people as many opportunities as possible so that they can come in contact with the books of Truth. Each person has the freedom to choose whether to realize or not realize the Truth, but the task of angels is, at the very least, to provide opportunities for enlightenment.

The Laws are not taught at every age. But when the Laws are taught, they are not only for people of that age. They are left for people who are coming 1,000, 2,000, or 3,000 years later so that they can also attain enlightenment. I publish a number of books one after another, and you are not the only readers I have in mind. In another 100 years, I will no longer be here on earth, but a part of my work is to enlighten those who will live 100 years later. What will the world be like 500 years from now? No matter how this world changes, the laws of the mind will not change. The Truth will not change. Our job is not to tell people of things that change. In this changing world, our mission is to awaken people to the Truth that will never change. In this age, what we teach may not be accepted by a great number of people. Even so, this teaching will become a guiding light for people who will come later. So we will never compromise with the norms of modern society. Even if times or environments change, no matter what kind of world unfolds, our mission is to point to what is unchanging in the midst of change. Knowing that this is our mission, we must have a broad perspective; we need to consider what we must leave behind for the new age to come—the Golden Age of the future. This is not my task alone but the task of every one of you also.

4

How Severe the Road to Enlightenment Is

However, the Laws are not fixed. The Laws in essence have one main pillar that connects to everything, and this pillar can rotate and radiate lights of different colors, like a prism. To receive the lights, we need to have the capacity to accept the light of each of these colors. In other words, certain teachings that some people may not need could be necessary for others. So the important point is how you accept the different lights of the Laws that are split through a "prism" and how you pass them on to others.

This means that you cannot just be a receiver. It means all of you here listening to me should not be content with just listening to me. If you've heard it, you must change your mind first. If you don't, you cannot say you have listened to my lecture; it only means my voice vibrated through your eardrums as mere sound. My words are not just sound. I am addressing every one of you; I am speaking to your souls. If my voice gives you a nostalgic feeling deep in your heart, this is because you have listened to my words before. It may not have been on earth; it may have been in the other world or past life on earth.

After this life, I will not reincarnate again for another 2,800 years. So there will not be another time I can speak to you with a physical body for the next 2,800 years. This being the case, my challenge is how effectively I can spend the remaining time I have left. This is my job. My mission is how well I can spend my time on earth, how far I can spread this Truth, and how many people it can reach. But it is not enough to simply spread the Truth far and wide. The real challenge is to provide teachings that can touch people's souls and to leave the teachings behind for generations to come.

To achieve this mission, I am not satisfied with just speaking through a loudspeaker on the street; the Laws cannot truly be passed on simply by meeting as many people as possible. Who was it that passed on Buddhism? It was the efforts of great monks who sought enlightenment. In the world of Truth, one person can have the power of ten thousand or even one million people. In an office, one person can only do the work of five people at most. But in the world of Truth, the value, influence, and way of life of one person are far greater. After I finish teaching various teachings, the torch of Truth will continue to illuminate people's lives if there is such a person every 10 or 20 years. This has been the basis of the transmission of Buddhism.

Now there are a lot of new religious groups or sects all over Japan. Officially, there are said to be 180,000, and if we include the ones that are not registered, there will be double or three times more. However, after the founders pass away, most of these groups are thrown into disarray and lose their momentum. Why does this happen? It happens because the successors are treating the founder's teachings like an inheritance. They inherit the teachings to protect their property, land, and daily life, seeing the teachings as if they are one of the estates of the deceased. But this attitude is a mistake. The Truth must be passed from one enlightened person to another. In history, Buddhism was transmitted from India to China and from China to Japan. Parental or sibling relationships were all meaningless when Buddha's teachings were passed down. The principle has always been "from one enlightened person to another."

You may have read *Spiritual Messages from Kukai*. Kukai traveled across the sea from Japan to China and studied the teachings under *Hui-kuo*, the seventh founder of Esoteric Buddhism (746–805) before he died. China is a foreign country to Japan. To the Chinese, Kukai was a monk who came to China from a foreign land. Kukai was a stranger. But Hui-Kuo entrusted the most important mission of passing on the torch of Truth to this foreigner, Kukai.

Can you imagine this now? There are many religions in Japan. But if a seeker of Truth came from Australia or maybe Canada, would any monk pass their torch of Truth to him or her? A monk may do so if the foreigner is willing to stay in Japan, but would any monk pass the torch of Truth to a foreigner who plans to go back to his or her home country?

As you can see, despite it being 1,200 years ago, the Chinese monk Hui-kuo was truly international and open-minded. He was able to make judgments from the standpoint of the Truth without having attachments to worldly things.

When Hui-kuo handed down the torch of Truth to Kukai before he passed away, I assume his Chinese disciples who were closest to him were very disappointed and envious. It seems they had a long discussion, thinking, "We followed Master Hui-kuo for a long time, but he did not select any of us to inherit his teachings. Instead, he chose a foreigner who stayed in China for only six months and left. This is not acceptable." However, this is what passing on the Laws means. This is how strict it is. The path of enlightenment can be likened to a ridgeway that connects the highest points of the mountains and is not a valley path. This path is not allowed to go down right to the bottom. The path must continue going from mountaintop to mountaintop, from ridge to ridge.

You must understand how strict it is to hand down the Laws. Personal consideration is completely unacceptable. Why? Because whether the Laws will be passed on correctly or if the true teachings will be passed on is the key to determining the happiness or unhappiness of not only the people of today but also the people of future generations. So when handing down the Laws, there are no compromises.

All of you who are studying the Laws must realize that you are undergoing spiritual discipline every day and you are standing at the edge of a cliff. It is as if you are confronting with a samurai sword that is pointing at you every day. Without such serious mindsets, how can you save future generations? Not only future generations, but how can you save the people of today? Even if our membership grows to ten thousand, one million, five million, or ten million people, if everyone who gathered acted like guests, it is meaningless. It is pointless. Instead, it will be more helpful for humankind if there are one or two people who have truly attained enlightenment. You need to understand this core idea in the spreading and succession of the Laws.

In Christianity, Paul the Apostle was a great missionary who is well known. His work and his actions were indeed great, but his lack of understanding of the Truth partly distorted the teachings of Christianity. He was not enlightened enough. This has cast a shadow over Christianity in its later stages and the life path of Christians. This cannot be forgiven. Saying it cannot be forgiven does not mean that you will fall to hell. It means that even if you did return to heaven, if there was 5 percent or even 10 percent of the Truth that you could not pass on correctly and that gets passed on to people for the next 2,000 years, then there is no turning back.

So you must all know that there is no end to learning the Laws. With all your intellect, with all your life, with all your passion, seek, seek, seek, seek, and keep seeking—even if you come to a realization, you must not let it satisfy you. Be aware of the possibility that there is more to it. Also, you must know that even if you hear my words, each of you will have a different understanding. Be aware of the consequences of passing it on with a different understanding. You must all be aware of these difficult realities of mastering the Laws and of seeking enlightenment.

Therefore, we must establish a foundation before we start missionary work. We are not doing this to put on a play or a show. Unless each of you becomes an angel or a pillar of light, what is the meaning of all this? Don't you agree? If so, go back to basics and check your awareness. When you think back about your awareness, can you say your enthusiasm and passion are enough? Please think about this. Could you be thinking in terms of mere gains and losses? Could you be thinking in terms of worldly pros and cons? Do you have a calculating mind? You must think about these things first.

I am not saying that you should be martyred on the cross like in Christianity. It doesn't matter if your physical body lives or dies. What I expect is this: Crucify the weakness in your mind that chooses the easy way. Crucify your mind that is easily swayed by worldly desires. Crucify the mind that is easily deluded by immediate worldly gain. This is the true meaning of the phrase, "Unless you are born again, you cannot see God, you cannot see spirits." It means you must once go through "death." Unless you have such a strong, unwavering, powerful resolve, you cannot truly absorb the Truth. You must first awaken yourself. You must first be awakened before you can awaken others.

5

Discover God within Yourself

At Happy Science, we receive many calls and letters from various religious groups. Some are threatening. They say that since Happy Science started its activities, their "business" has declined and that we are harming their business. But these people do not realize that we are acting with indomitable determination. Their motivation is to protect their profits in this world only, but we are working to protect God's will. In time, they will come to understand that our objectives are different. Will they be able to make a living? Will their group survive? Will their staff be able to receive a salary? None of this matters. We cannot distort the Truth for such reasons. The Truth is the Truth, and what is right is right. God's will is God's will. Without communicating this, I cannot complete my mission as a trumpet of God.

Kanzo Uchimura, the Japanese Christian leader (1861–1930), declared, "I will fight all enemies of the Truth." My feelings are exactly the same as him except about one point. In my view, there are no enemies of the Truth in this world. On earth, no one is the enemy of the Truth. People are either awakened to the Truth or are yet to awaken to the Truth. We have no enemies. You must realize that on this earth, there are no devils, nor is there any evil of real substance. What may appear to stand against us are not truly evil existences. They are not bad people, demons, or satans. They are simply existences that have not yet awakened to the Truth. They, too, are children of God. It is not about whether they are good or bad people. It is just the difference between people who have removed the scales from their eyes and people who still have scales on their eyes. God did not create humans as incomplete beings.

We should learn the spirit of Kanzo Uchimura—"fighting all enemies of the Truth"—but we must know that the Truth has no enemies. If there are no enemies, then everyone is your ally. Some are active supporters, whereas others have yet to realize that they should be supporting our movement. A hundred million people in Japan have scales on their eyes. There are only a few hundred, a few thousand, or tens of thousands of people who have awakened to the Truth (at the time of the lecture). We are not going to fight against an enemy but rather are reminding people of the true Laws and rekindling the torch in their hearts. We must have firm determination to advance on our path. We will neither fight nor compromise; we will confidently watch over the Truth unfolding itself on earth. This attitude is important. This indomitable spirit is important.

The foundation for this attitude is the belief that love has no enemies. No matter how hard a person's shell of self-protection may be, it can never be hard enough to shield them against the spear of love. So when we act, we have to strive to find each person's divine nature—the brilliance of the diamond that shines in every single person's individuality. This brilliance of the diamond is the same brilliance that you will discover within yourself as you polish your soul. To love others means to love the sacred radiance that shines within them. It is to love their true nature, which is the nature of a child of God. This divine nature in others is in fact the same nature that you have within yourself. This is the true meaning of the saying, "you and others are one." God discovers God. A child of God discovers a child of God. A child of God loves a child of God. You need to treat others with this perspective.

This being so, what does it mean to attain enlightenment? First, it means to discover the divine nature within you. Only those who have discovered their divine inner nature can see the divine nature in others. Those who have yet to discover their divine inner nature will not be able to see others' divine inner nature, let alone help them to discover it. So Hinayana should not be separate from Mahayana. We must understand that the seed of the Mahayana already exists in Hinayana. In *The Golden Laws*, I explained that "benefiting yourself benefits others," or "benefit yourself first and, in that process, benefit others," is the essence of Shakyamuni Buddha's teaching. To benefit yourself here does not mean to protect your own ego or your own interests. It is the path to make your divine nature shine and also find others' divine nature that resonates with the light within you. You must know that this teaching does not separate you from others.

6

Exploration of the Right Mind and Principle of Happiness

Now we need to talk about how to find our inner light: God within. As you have already read and heard in my books and lectures, I started Happy Science with the teachings of the "Exploration of the Right Mind" and the "Principle of Happiness." I have taught that the exploration of the Right Mind is the entrance and the way out of the Truth; it is the pillar that runs through your spiritual discipline on earth and also the lifeline that connects you to God. God gave every person a lifeline to keep us from drowning in the deep delusional ocean called this world. This lifeline is the practice called the exploration of the Right Mind. So it means that you should master the Right Mind.

What then is the Right Mind? In my books, such as *Shin Kokoro no Tankyu* (lit. "The Exploration of the Mind: New Version"), I talked about the state of mind from various angles. The righteousness I speak of is not about rightness in the sense of the duality of right and wrong. It is the value that appears as you dig deeper and search for something true. This is what righteousness is. It is what shines brighter and brighter as you explore and search deeper and harder. This is the righteousness I am talking about now.

In this sense, this righteousness is not black and white, like precepts that say, "You may do this, and you may not do that." In the past, many guiding spirits descended to earth and left various precepts that stated what people can and cannot do, such as "you shall not kill," "you shall not steal," and "you shall not bear false witness." Moses was one of these spirits and Shakyamuni was another. They gave commandments and precepts and indicated certain rules that practitioners must keep. But those rules were not given to distinguish right from wrong. They served as a kind of fence to protect seekers from straying from the path of enlightenment. They were like guideposts. We must transcend the duality of righteousness, just thinking in terms of right and wrong, and have the courage to discover the brilliance of the Truth in all and everything. The Truth is not to be found in a simplistic set of rules of conduct, such as "if you do this and that, you will go to heaven, and if you break this precept, you will go to hell." Rather, you need to know that the precepts were made only to prevent practitioners from going astray in the earlier stages.

Even if a person leaves this world without having killed a single mosquito or ant, it does not mean he or she will be held in high regard in the real world. Even if someone has killed a mosquito, if he or she has saved, guided, and nurtured thousands of people, righteousness will be on that person's side. Rather than becoming a good-but-weak person bound by precepts, we need the courage to seek and explore the righteousness hidden deep within everyone and everything. We are not "religious" people. We are the captain and the crew who set sail on the ocean in search of the Truth. It does not matter if we are a religion or not. We are now sailing the ocean of the Truth with the same spirit as Columbus, who set out to sea 500 years ago and discovered a new continent. On earth, there may not be any sea or land that has not been investigated. The question is: which direction should seekers of Truth head toward? The answer is the world beyond earth, the world of God, the real world. You must realize that you are "scientists" and "explorers." You must change your perspective and your way of thinking. You must know that you are Magellans and Columbuses. You must know that you are modern-day Galileos. You must know that you are modern-day Copernicuses. In this sense, you must know that the exploration of the spiritual world is science itself that explores from the present into the future. Science is essentially a field of research into the unknown. This spirit is the basis of Happy Science.

Now that you have learned that the exploration of righteousness, the exploration of the Right Mind, is a lifeline to God, the next question is: what is the principle of happiness? On March 8, 1987, at Ushigome Public Hall, I explained in the lecture: "Love, wisdom, self-reflection, and progress are the modern Fourfold Path and the path to modern enlightenment. The exploration and mastery of these four paths is the principle of happiness. The happiness we teach is not just happiness in this world or the other world only but happiness in both this world and the other world."

You must know that your true path to happiness is also the path to enlightenment. The happiness we talk about is the happiness of attaining enlightenment. So then what does it mean to attain enlightenment? It means to realize the true nature of humans who reincarnate between this and the other world and to know how humans are expected to live. It is to understand (the nature of) not only the three-dimensional world that we are training in now but also the real world, such as the fourth, fifth, sixth, seventh, eighth, and ninth dimensions created by God. This is why "knowing leads to enlightenment, and enlightenment is the same as happiness."

What great happiness it is to know everything. In this world, no matter how affluent you are, no matter how high your social status is, you are unhappy unless you know where you came from and where you are going and can reflect on your lifestyle from the perspective of God. No matter how much fortune you make, you cannot take your bank accounts to the other world. You cannot take your status with you. What you can take to the other world is a pure mind, a Right Mind, and a true mind. That is all. That is why you must explore your Right Mind and thoroughly practice the four principles: love, wisdom, self-reflection, and progress; these are the practical expressions of exploring the Right Mind. This path is how we should live, incorporating the Hinayana and Mahayana teachings.

7

Without Self-reflection there Is No Enlightenment

In the lecture in May 1987, I talked about the principle of love. I explained that "Love is based on the wisdom of acknowledging equality but also on the wisdom of acknowledging differences. It has stages. It shows us the goal of our efforts and the path of our training." In the same year in July, at Koganei Public Hall, my lecture was on the principle of the mind. I focused on the exploration of the Right Mind.

Now, the title of this lecture is "The Principle of Enlightenment." What I am teaching about is the meaning of the principle of self-reflection of the Fourfold Path. The fundamental principle of Happy Science begins by talking about the principle of happiness as an introduction, followed by the principle of love. Then comes the principle of the mind, followed by this lecture on the principle of enlightenment. Eventually, in December 1987, I will talk about the principle of progress, and in the spring of 1988, the principle of wisdom. I changed the order of the lectures from that of the Fourfold Path, but I plan to give talks on the basic structure of the Laws within a year. Here, in this lecture, "The Principle of Enlightenment," I have to eventually reach the principle of self-reflection and how to practice self-reflection.

So what is self-reflection? Earlier, I said knowing is the first step to attaining enlightenment. The reason I said human beings tend to take the easy way and live as they please is that they are content with the way they live. This being so, you need to acquire knowledge of the Truth to be able to look back on your life and see yourself objectively through the eyes of a third person, as if you are examining yourself through a transparent glass box. This is essential. This knowledge of how God's light unfolds will become light or a mirror in which you can see yourself. The principle of self-reflection asks you to begin by knowing and then to explore deeper and deeper into your inner self.

Please think. Before you encountered the Truth, had you ever reflected on your thoughts or deeds? You may have been taught the importance of self-reflection as part of your moral education at school or home. But no one probably taught you that the principle of self-reflection is a way of exploring and finding your true nature as a child of God and the true way of attaining enlightenment. In India, 2,600 years ago, the teachings of Shakyamuni began with self-reflection and ended with self-reflection. It was the starting point.

After we are born into this world, we grow up in a family, receive an education from our parents and school, and are influenced by our friends and society. As a consequence, for better or for worse, we are "dyed" and "tainted" by different colors and live our lives "wearing colored costumes." However, people are unaware that they are wearing colored costumes. Everyone wants to lead a wonderful life, but unfortunately, many people are dyeing themselves gray through the way they live. This is why we need self-reflection. This is what "laundry of the mind" means.

We did not come into this world wearing dirty clothes; the original "fabric" of our minds was truly clean and pure. However, within 20, 30, 40, or 50 years, our minds become stained with different colors during our lives. People whose minds are directed toward what is right are in brilliant heavenly colors, whereas those who are living mistakenly change to a dark gray color. You need to realize that you are living on earth unaware of this fact. Pitiful are the people who do not know how much their current self has changed from their original state of mind. This is a very sad way of leading your life. So the first step in self-reflection is to know how much your mind has distanced from God's will.

8

Progress and Harmony

What should we do after we become aware of the distance? The next step is to come closer to our original state. What is the method for doing this? There are various methods, such as the Eightfold Path and the Six Paramitas of Buddhism. However, the basis of every method is essentially the same.

Broadly speaking, the basic principle of enlightenment has two principles—the principle of progress and the principle of harmony. The principle of progress aims to achieve self-improvement and development through individual efforts—this is one aspect of enlightenment. Another aspect of enlightenment is the principle of harmony. Check to see that you are not hurting others while you are improving yourself and that you are contributing to the happiness of many. If I use the analogy of trees, the trees that grow in a way that harms other trees have to be cut down. For trees to grow together, each tree must grow straight up toward the sky. If some trees grow at an angle, arching toward the ground or twisting, then they will stop others from growing healthily. Each tree is allowed to grow, but its growth must not harm others; otherwise, there will not be true happiness. So we must aim for harmony as we progress.

What is behind these two principles of progress and harmony? The basis for the principle of harmony is the idea that every human being is a child of God, so everyone is equal. Everyone is equal in the sense that we all originate from God, and we are all of equal value. This view of equality is the origin of the principle of harmony. What then is the idea behind the principle of progress? Although everyone starts equal, people are impartially rewarded by results that correspond to their efforts. So the principle of progress can be described as a principle of fairness.

For this great universe to develop and prosper, both the values of progress and harmony or fairness and equality must be realized. At the starting point, everyone is equal. Everyone is equal in terms of their potential for progress; we are all equally promised limitless progress. However, depending on the effort that each person makes, it becomes unequal. You need to know that the Laws that govern this universe compromise two perspectives—"equality and differentiation" or "equality and fairness."

Although everyone, as a child of God, is promised infinite progress, some people work hard while others do not, and some people advance while others regress. To reward everyone equally would be far from justice. The results you get will be according to the efforts you make and on how you bear the fruits of the seeds that you sow. This is known as the rule of cause and effect or the rule of action and reaction. There are various names to this rule, but they all state that you will get the results that correspond to your actions. This is the same idea as the principle of fairness.

Shakyamuni once said that Buddha-nature is to be found in everyone and everything, be it mountains, rivers, grass, trees, or land. This is the idea of equality. But at the same time, he also taught that enlightenment has stages. It leads to the idea of fairness, which is another principle. If there is a cause, a corresponding result will come to fruition. Even a good leader or an angel will suffer accordingly if he or she strays from the path, whereas those who have made an ordinary start will receive God's blessings accordingly if they have made achievements through continued effort.

We first need to understand that these two principles are the basis of happiness and the basis of enlightenment. This being so, we only have one direction to go. Every human being is a child of God and has the same Buddha-nature. But as long as Buddha-nature manifests in different stages, we must keep striving to improve ourselves while loving all things and respecting equality in all things. This is the principle of enlightenment. One of the ways is to remove the clouds or stains from your mind, restore its original brilliance, and then courageously take the step toward making many people happy while building a noble character. This principle does not apply to you only. This applies equally to me as well.

Be courageous and take the first step toward further self-improvement. Let's work hard together!

CHAPTER FIVE

The Principle of Progress

The Fifth Public Lecture of 1987

Originally recorded in Japanese on December 20, 1987
at Japan Municipal Research Center in Tokyo, Japan
and later translated into English.

1

Progress that Comes
Only After Self-reflection

In this lecture, I will talk about the principle of progress. The progress I teach at Happy Science is the progress that comes only after self-reflection—the progress that starts from self-reflection. In other words, when I say the words prosperity or progress, I do not mean prosperity or progress that is built on sand. We started our movement by establishing a strong foundation. This is how we have established our basic stance of "Build the foundation and then the pillars" or "First strengthen the inside, then the outside." These are not just a part of our teachings but also the guiding principles of our activities.

This world is full of people who want to create an ideal world. Of course, they are not necessarily people in religion but also people in politics, business, the arts, and cultural movements. There are people in various fields who are working with a wish to create some kind of utopia on earth. But many of them end up giving rise to confusion and making mistakes. Why does this happen? One reason is that even though they have high ideals, they are not down to earth. Some examples of such people (in Japan) include student activists or members of the United Red Army (a far-left group), who gave rise to certain incidents. They, too, are aiming to build a wonderful society based on their ideals, but they are mistaken in attempting to save and lead others before they have established themselves. This is a major problem.

This idea of first establishing oneself is not new. In China, 2,500 years ago, Confucius taught people the process of first mastering themselves and how it eventually leads to building a wonderful society. In India, Gautama Siddhartha, the Shakyamuni Buddha, also taught the same principle 2,600 years ago. He also began by teaching people to first work on establishing themselves. Many of his disciples rushed to spread Buddha's teachings because they thought, "We have found the true teachings, so now we must tell other people and spread them right away." But at that time, Buddha held them back and said to them, "Do not rush. You must polish yourself first. There is no end to how much you can improve yourself. You must spend your life improving yourself. Know yourself. Know your shortcomings. When you preach to someone without doing this, know that you have already become arrogant. Beware of this. Remember to always look within. The moment you forget to self-reflect is the beginning of spiritual degradation." This is what Shakyamuni Buddha said to his disciples.

Since Happy Science began, I have met and observed many people, listened to their opinions, and read what they wrote. What I realized is that the most difficult time for people is when they are about to take a leap, about to succeed, and about to be recognized by people. This is a very difficult time for the seekers of Truth. Yet this difficult time is actually the first hurdle. Unless you overcome this hurdle, unless you get through this strait gate, the road to enlightenment will not open up before you. That is why we must always reflect on ourselves. People are easily carried away by success. This applies not only to you but also to me and the people around me.

We have already published 28 books and printed over 500,000 copies (as of December 1987), but this is just a single milestone. Our goal is not only to awaken 120 million Japanese people to the Truth. Our goal is to awaken people all over the world and to leave behind nourishment for the souls of the people that will come 500, 1,000, 2,000, or 3,000 years from now. If so, it is important for us to deeply understand that we have only taken the first step forward in achieving our goal.

To stop myself from becoming conceited, I have set a goal to publish 1,000 books of Truth within the several decades I have remaining in this lifetime (as of October 2021, more than 2,900 books have been published). So far, I have published 28 books, so I have 972 more books to go. I have only just begun. In Japan, there are 120 million people. Among them, there are only tens of thousands of people who have read my books and just a few thousand people who have become members (as of December 1987). We still have a long way to go, so we cannot let ourselves get caught up by such small successes. We have to remind ourselves of where we are at this moment.

I'm sure many of you here are highly advanced souls. The more advanced you are and the older your soul is, the more carefully you need to reflect on yourself. Do not become conceited. Do not become proud of yourself so easily. Do not regard yourself as a great figure so easily. If you are great, you would produce results befitting your greatness. So please remember the following perspective: "If I haven't produced my desired results, it means I'm not so great yet. But I have the possibility to become great."

2

Progress through the Middle Way

So the title of today's lecture is "The Principle of Progress." In the previous lecture, "The Principle of Enlightenment," I mentioned a few points about self-reflection. Put simply, in the laws of progress, which I am about to discuss, the progress is that found in the Middle Way. The progress that is found in the Middle Way is a way of thinking that does not hurt others or yourself. This way of thinking embraces infinite possibilities for development and progress.

If so, before you make any progress, you must enter the Middle Way. To enter the Middle Way, you must avoid falling to the extremes and deviating from the middle. What does it mean to avoid falling to the extremes? Let us discuss this. By avoiding the extremes, I do not mean you must drive straight ahead without turning the steering wheel. In the course of your life, there are times when you need to turn left or right. You can turn when necessary, but each time you do, you must remember to bring the steering wheel back to the center. This is what it means. A great mistake will occur when you don't. You are not a robot or a roller coaster that just runs on a track. You are a noble soul who has been allowed to think and act with free will. You are God's great creation and endowed with the utmost freedom. Because you have been given such freedom, you need to think of a way you can correct yourself if you lose track in the course of your life, master the way, and put it into practice.

Now, let us discuss the mindset and the way of thinking to live by to enter the Middle Way. We cannot spend our days just meditating in a cave because we are all a part of society and have responsibilities. So the question is how people can live by the Middle Way while being a part of society and being around other people. Also, what does it mean to avoid the two extremes? We must think about this.

Here are some examples of the extremes. One is to think and act in a way that is clearly harmful to others, such as through anger. Anger is a typical checkpoint for self-reflection. How often do you get angry? There are religious leaders who are held in high regard, but some of them still fly into a rage when their pride is hurt. This is because they do not yet know the real meaning of spiritual discipline. To not become angry is actually the starting point of spiritual discipline.

Then, why do people get angry or upset? It happens when people see the other person not acting according to the way they want them to. Anger arises automatically when expectations are not fulfilled. However, not getting angry is the most basic level of spiritual discipline: it is the basic of the basics. For the past 10 years, I haven't become angry once. How is this possible? It is because the moment

I feel anger welling up from within, I make the effort to see and understand the situation from both the other person's and my own perspective as well as from a third-person perspective. This must be done in an instant. When people become angry and say harmful things to others, they have already lost control of their minds and are only thinking about themselves. If they could spare a moment to consider the feelings of others, the situation would be different. Also, if they could widen their perspective and imagine a third person watching them, they can discover yet another viewpoint. Or instead of a third person, if you think that the high spirits in heaven are watching, things will be different. What is more, if people can think God is watching, trivial anger will disappear. So, regarding anger, as the first step of your spiritual discipline, I ask you to make efforts to instantaneously change your perspective.

Jealousy or envy is another example of emotion. For the seekers of Truth, how they control their feelings of jealously or envy is an important key point in their spiritual disciple. What causes people to feel jealous? Jealousy arises when people come across somebody who seems more highly regarded by society or a specific individual than they are and their pride is wounded. Why does it hurt? It hurts because when people perceive someone else who is valued higher or is more loved than them, they automatically feel less loved in comparison. They are in pain because they feel less loved, and this feeling is what sets jealousy aflame in their heart.

However, the seekers of Truth must strive to change this way of thinking. That is because jealousy is an emotion that destroys not only others but also yourself. Everyone has an ideal self-image deep within. The feeling of jealousy is essentially a feeling of wanting to bring people down. This person you are trying to bring down is, in truth, already the embodiment of your ideal self-image. Deep down, you want to be like that person. But the person who has realized your ideal self-image is not you but somebody else, so it makes you want to destroy that person. In short, when you harbor jealously against someone, you are actually also hurting your ideal self-image or the seed to becoming your ideal self. When you are jealous of someone, you are pulling yourself away from becoming your ideal self at a subconscious level. You will essentially be moving away from that ideal and going in the opposite direction. This is why you should overcome jealousy to not hurt yourself as well as others.

How can you overcome jealousy? The first point is that other people cannot help you overcome it. People with jealousy tend to attribute the cause of their problems to other people. They think they've done nothing wrong and that others are to blame. They strongly think so. But the problem lies within themselves; they are the ones creating a narrow mind that cannot accept others who are held in higher regard. What makes people narrow-minded? It is essentially the lack of self-trust or confidence. These people do not trust themselves. Why is this? This is because they know very well that they have not achieved anything worthy of recognition from many people.

In spite of that, they still want praise, and it creates a gap between their ideal and the reality. How can people overcome this gap? To close this gap, some people take the easy way out. There are usually two ways. The first is to try and draw attention to themselves in this world, for example, by appearing on television, getting their name known, or doing something that makes them stand out. They try to satisfy their need by making their name and face known in this world. This is one way. Another way is to be recognized in a world away from this world. People who choose this option have already given up on worldly success, but they still have hope of becoming famous in the world of Truth or the world of religion. Even if they are regarded as incompetent in their workplace, they still have hope of standing in the spotlight and gaining respect within a spiritual group and of possibly discovering that they are an angel or a tathagata. Some people have come to Happy Science just for this reason.

However, these people need to think twice. The cause of their jealousy does not lie externally. It lies within them. If they are confident with themselves, what other people think or say about them does not matter. This knowledge of their own shallowness makes them want to compensate for it. So what should these people do? I have been providing various answers to this question in my teachings. One way is to continue spiritual discipline diligently, day after day. The accumulation of daily effort is very important. Do not think that negative feelings, including a sense of inferiority, can be overcome in one leap. Also, do not think that small successes can ease it immediately. You should have an unshakable mind and observe yourself calmly even in the midst of praise or censure from others. Please remember to strive to become such a person.

3

Start from Acknowledging Yourself as Ordinary

I have spoken about various things. But in terms of how I see myself, I have never thought I am outstanding. I am ordinary by nature, and I started from the ordinary. I have never found abilities of mine to be superior to those of other people. I just always knew that "I am an ordinary person." What I then realized was that this awareness of being ordinary was actually the key to becoming extraordinary.

The world is full of talented people. Both men and women here—I believe many of whom go to work—must have met people who appear flawless. There is usually one person like this in every office—someone who is sharp-minded, good at talking to people, and fast at work, or someone who is good at golf and karaoke, can hold their liquor and is liked by women. These people just seemed to be capable of anything. Every section in a company has such a person who is good at everything, and such people are constantly trying to show off. Many of you probably feel inferior around them.

I, myself, have met such people and have worked with them. I had feelings of envy when I started working with such people, but after a while, that feeling subsided. That is because I understood that all they were doing is using their attributes to make themselves look good. In other words, they find comfort in being told they are great and cannot be at ease unless they are recognized as such. Such kinds of people are actually very lonely deep down. They always want to be recognized more and more and feel that they are not recognized enough. So they try to make themselves look almighty or multi-talented. I've met people like this, but they didn't impress me. Of course, I felt I couldn't be like them even if I tried, but the reason why they didn't impress me was that something was insincere about them. They were insincere in how they didn't want anyone to see their flaws and protected themselves from being seen by other people. They were living and working while covering themselves in such a kind of hard shell. The minds of these people are turbulent and full of anxiety and irritation.

Because I was an ordinary person since birth, I can let go of things very quickly. In other words, my policy is to know my own strength and to not force myself when something falls outside of it. Of course, it is important for people to have general knowledge of many things; they need to broaden their perspectives and gain experiences. However, I often see people who are "good at everything" leading dismal lives in their later years. That is because they lived the kind of life everyone else would admire and applaud but did not choose the path they themselves are satisfied with. When I see such people, I remind myself of how essential it is to lead a life that you are happy with rather than a life that draws people's admiration. So it is important to learn to know your limits and let go of some of your abilities.

Some of you might be disappointed hearing this in a lecture on the principle of progress, but this is what will actually help you progress. Everyone is given just 24 hours in a day; it is the same for you and me and for everyone in this world, whether you are American, Chinese, African, or European. We all only have 24 hours in a day. Also, people rarely live for more than 100 years. But it is true that when you get up each morning, you have 24 hours "densely packed in your wallet." Everyone is given the same amount of time, and we live for such a limited amount of time. As long as we live under such conditions, we cannot aim to become an "almighty god."

There have been geniuses such as Leonardo da Vinci, but very few people can live as he did. So we must start with the awareness that we are ordinary people. You may wonder if you are a reincarnation of an angel or if you are a soul who was created in the very distant past. These thoughts might be useful for inspiring enthusiasm, but starting with an awareness of being ordinary is also important. Only when you start from the ordinary can you build your life steadily.

4

Applying the Middle Way to Modern Life

80/20 thinking

Some of you may wonder how studying the Truth will be advantageous for your work and life. Just like the example I gave earlier, some people might think that to get promoted in a company, they need to socialize with many people and be able to stay up all night playing mahjong or drink every night. So they might assume that such physical toughness is necessary for success. But what I recommend is to start with an awareness of being ordinary. You must be aware that you only have 24 hours in a day and that you have limited abilities. Therefore, you should concentrate on what truly resonates with your soul and what accords with your inner ideals. If you think you have unlimited talent, then this is not a problem for you. But if you don't feel this way, it is essential to allocate your supply of limited time on what you believe to be most important or meaningful. This is the key to a successful life.

As I've said in previous seminars, I used to work for a trading company, so I had various occasions for socializing. What I can say is that it is very important to not become too absorbed in certain matters. In the last few years, my main interest has been the study of the mind and providing teachings of the mind. This being so, I needed to use 80 percent of my time and energy for the study of the mind and the remaining 20 percent for experiencing other things. This has been my policy. I used 20 percent of the remaining time and energy to gain experiences that I could not have when I was in seclusion.

I'm sure some of my readers enjoy playing golf and are competing against one another in terms of how many handicaps you have—whether you are a single-digit handicapper, 10 handicapper, or 20 handicapper. You may be surprised to hear this but I also played golf at one time. But I did not immerse myself in it—it was a question of how far I took it. For example, businessmen (in Japan) usually play golf once a month during spring, summer, and early autumn for socialization purposes. There are certain work-related social obligations that employees have to attend to. But of course, people do not want to use up an entire day. Then, what should we do? The only thing you can do is try not to immerse yourself in socializing. In golf, your ability is measured by handicap indexes. My golf handicap was around 30, which means I was just a beginner. When I played a few rounds with my colleagues, I could just about get one or two handicaps over them, and that was the best I could do at the time, so I accepted it and left it at that.

I also played mahjong during my trading company days—I've played it, but I didn't continue playing it. After I tried it one or two times, I came up with an excuse so that I can stop playing it. When I was in New York, I played mahjong against an American colleague and lost. Since then, I have been using it as an excuse. I would just say, "I am deeply ashamed as a Japanese businessman to lose to an American and swore never to play again." Ever since, I was able to make time in the evening. Like so, there are various methods you can use.

The same applies to other sports. In my high school days, I practiced kendo, a Japanese martial art, and reached the rank of first-*dan*. I continued it in university, and I could have advanced to an even higher rank—second-*dan* or third-*dan*—had I wanted to. But when I compared the amount of time I would spend practicing kendo with that I would spend on my other activities, I decided to quit once I reached first-*dan* and did not try to advance further. However, at the time, I was showing the skills of a second- and third-*dan* player in competitions.

I played tennis, too, and was the captain of the company tennis team. We used to play once a month, but, again, I did not delve deeply into it. I was chosen as the captain because of my leadership abilities; it's not as if I had a history of winning tournaments. So on my team, the captain was the least reliable in matches; I could swing a racket and hit the ball, but it would sometimes go out of the court, so my skills weren't enough. But I became the captain because I had the skills to keep people engaged. I was also able to raise money for the tennis club. Whenever I would negotiate with the human resources and general affairs departments, they would allocate more money for us, so I was appointed the captain for two years simply for my natural character. I was happy to do it, as my presence had a positive effect on 40–50 people on the team, and they were happy to have me as the captain. As long as I was around, the club had a big enough budget and our request for an offsite training camp was always approved. People appreciated my presence, and I was supposedly the embodiment of love incarnate for them. So I appeared on the tennis court once a month. (In actuality, my skill level was high enough to be considered a C-level professional tennis coach.) In this way, I have tried many things, but I took control and stopped once I reached a certain level and didn't get myself deeply involved. This was my way.

Many (Japanese) people working in sales have to socialize with colleagues and customers after work. If you take it too seriously, you would be out from Monday to Friday, and you will be seen as a loser if you don't go. I have a low tolerance for alcohol. I can only drink a small-sized bottle of beer. If it is whisky mixed with water, two glasses was my limit. So when I had no choice but to go out at night—from about seven in the evening to three in the morning—I would spend eight hours topping up my glass with ice cubes to make it look like I was drinking.

In this way, I've used many techniques, and I have never tried to be a person that was good at everything; at the same time, I did not try to live a life where I am completely unsociable and out of the norm. It is important to put 80 percent of your energy into your main mission and the other 20 percent into gaining other experiences. This was my policy. With the 20 percent, I expanded my experience but did not involve myself too deeply in activities I was not very good at. There are many other things I have tried, but the key here is to keep focusing on your main mission. This is important. Once you keep doing this, you will be on your way to boundless success.

So how will this lead to success? People will make continual efforts toward something they find most valuable. They can tirelessly devote 5, 10, or 20 years to it. On the other hand, if they feel something is meaningless, they cannot do it for so long. Therefore, if you are aware that you have limited abilities, you must discover the most brilliant part, the most attractive part, the most wonderful part of your soul to succeed. You must not turn away from it. You must not turn away from bringing out the best in you. Because there are only 24 hours in a day, it is sensible to think about how to use these hours to live the best life possible. This is one of the modern practical applications of the Middle Way I am teaching you in this lecture.

If people think, "Now that I have Happy Science, I will only study the Truth and nothing else as I live in this society," that is not the right way to live. You might be able to protect your inner kingdom by concentrating only on the Truth, but you will lose the opportunity to be influenced by the people you meet or to be an influence to them. It is not desirable for one to live as a lonely philosopher; if you wanted to live that way, you could have just meditated in the heavenly world. Yet you are here in this world, so that means you have something to learn through your relationships with others. So the more you refine yourself, the greater influence you should have on others. You may have experiences that seem like a waste of time, but it is important to grasp the ones among them that polish your soul.

If you spend 100 percent of your time on things you are not really interested in, that is foolish. But it is also not right to spend 100 percent of your time on only your own interests because you will lose the opportunity to influence others. As for me, I have been giving a lecture once every two months. Ideally, I want to meet more and more people and talk about a lot of things. My wish is to meet and talk to as many people as I can. However, the idea of the Middle Way applies to my present lifestyle, too. I do not spend 100 percent of my time on myself, nor do I spend it on others only. I secure enough time for myself, and I always like to make opportunities to meet as many people as possible to influence them and to be influenced by them.

I currently spend 80 percent of my time refining myself and the remaining 20 percent meeting other people. Perhaps this ratio seems strange to you. You may think that if I really wished to convey the Truth and save as many people as possible, this ratio is wrong; you may think I should be meeting and talking to as many people as I can and working myself to the bone every day. However, this idea can be compared to a sprinter. You might be able to run 100 meters at top speed, but at that pace, you will not be able to finish the long-distance marathon called life. It is therefore important to develop yourself first and gradually become a more influential person.

Developing "the part of the iceberg that lies underwater"

Happy Science will continue to grow in members, and my lecture audience will grow to 2,000, 3,000, 4,000, or 5,000 people (as of 2021, I have given lectures at venues in front of 50,000 people many times). So I must think of teachings that I can preach to a large number of people when the time comes. This is what it means to live while always looking ahead to the future. Within your 24 hours, it is very important that you do not expend all your time and energy thinking about the present only but make time for planning and preparations for the future. As a person with a mission to teach people how to live, no matter how hard I study and think deeply about the human mind or my own mind, it is never enough. There is no end.

The same goes for you, too. Some of our members have been awarded top scores in Happy Science seminars or examinations. These people scored over 90 points. The full score is set at 100 points on these tests, but it could be different from God's point of view. Their 90 points could be out of 100,000, 1 million, or 100 million. We do not know. So it is important that you do not just think about how many points away you are from the full score. You must know that there is a vast world you need to explore beyond that.

What I am trying to say is that although you are now filled with passion for conveying the joy of knowing the Truth to as many people as possible, you must remember to apply the ideas of accumulation and recharge your lives. If you forget this, you will have feelings of inferiority, jealousy, and anger. When you expose 100 percent of yourself, you will be too influenced by others' opinions of you. Instead, like an iceberg, try to show only a portion of yourself to others; only 10-20 percent of yourself is enough. For the remaining 80-90 percent, you should delve deeply into your inner world and establish the self that is not seen by others. This part of you below the surface will help weigh you down so that you can withstand the rough waves of life. If the whole of you is floating above the surface, it will cause you to sway back and forth, from one extreme to the other. You must not think too much about the self that is above the surface. Rather, have confidence in the self that is underneath, below the surface. You must have confidence in the self that is not evaluated by others.

Now ask yourself sincerely: How much of you is below the surface? When you take away the part that is exposed or the part that others praise you for, what is left? What remains after your job is removed from you? What remains after your family is removed from you? If you take away the parts of you that others praise you for, what are you left with? Please think about these things. The larger the base that is not seen by others—the part under the water—becomes, the bigger the iceberg will be. Wind or waves will not affect you. This is how you can develop an unshakable mind. This process of building the self below the surface is one of the ways of entering the Middle Way. You must remember this.

Do you not get angry or jealous, have hatred, or complain about people's words and speak ill of them because almost all of you is exposed to others? Do you not feel that way because you lack confidence in the self that is visible to other people? Do you think you will become emotional or hostile toward others if you have absolute confidence in the 80-90 percent of yourself that is not seen by other people? People who easily get emotional are usually selfish individuals who constantly think only about themselves. If they truly care about themselves, they should cultivate their inner self. They should build a greater self in the part that is not seen by other people.

I said earlier that one of the ways of entering the Middle Way in the world today is to use 80 percent of your energy on the areas you are most interested in and the remaining 20 percent on gaining a variety of other experiences. Another method—which is actually the same method explained differently—is to develop the "underwater part of the iceberg." This is one way of stabilizing your life and entering the Middle Way. In other words, it is important for you to build a firm foundation in your life. With this, you will be able to withstand all kinds of winds and waves you may encounter.

Keep moving forward

What is the third way of entering the Middle Way? What kind of thinking is the third way? My advice is, "Keep moving forward." This can be explained by how a bicycle works. When you first tried to ride a bicycle, you probably wondered how on earth people could ride such an unstable vehicle. You may have thought, "How can I possibly sit on this and ride it when there are only two narrow wheels? Why was such a vehicle invented? Normally, there have to be four wheels or at least three for it to be stable. Yet a bicycle only has two wheels and somehow people are actually able to ride it. Who invented such a thing? How can people mount a bicycle and ride it straight?"

A bicycle will fall as soon as it stops, but as long as it is moving, it will stay upright. This is where the secret is. To prevent yourself from swaying from left to right in life, you need to always keep on moving forward. Only when you know you are always moving forward can you avoid going to the extremes and enter the Middle Way. You cannot enter the Middle Way by sitting still and doing nothing all day. As the name "Middle Way" suggests, the way is to keep moving forward.

I have introduced three methods of entering the Middle Way: the first is the 80/20 thinking, the second is to work on the self that is beneath the surface and is not judged by others, and the third is to keep moving forward. This is the modern interpretation of entering the Middle Way explained simply to help you understand this concept.

5

Entering the Middle Way
Through Self-reflection

Self-reflection is to remove the "dirt"

Apart from these methods, there is a traditional method of entering the Middle Way—through self-reflection. There are countless methods and checkpoints for self-reflection. Ideally, individualized one-on-one guidance is necessary. As I have said repeatedly, self-reflection does not mean seeing yourself as a sinful child. It is not about telling yourself to observe the hopeless self that is covered in dust, nor is it about telling yourself to do something about this self. When you reflect on yourself, you must not forget that your true nature that shines brilliantly like a diamond lies deep within you. This perspective is one of the important aspects of the self-reflection that I teach.

Self-reflection does not mean just eradicating all the evil within you. It is not based on the idea that human beings are born as sinners. It is not about telling yourself to just correct your mistakes. Self-reflection reminds you of the wonderful self you have deep within you; it reminds you of the diamond in your core. You are one with the high spirits through this diamond, and it serves as a pipe that connects you and God.

You have this golden pipeline within. Always remember this. Through this golden pipeline you have within, light flows from high spirits into you. So, first, you need to understand this nature you have. Then, based on this knowledge, you should remove the dirt on the outside of the pipe.

So the purpose of self-reflection that I teach is not to make you feel miserable or be self-abusive. Through self-reflection, you should feel clean and light, as if you have just come out of the shower. You need to recognize that you are truly warm, clear-minded, kind, and marvelous. After practicing self-reflection, you should start radiating light. If you only see your shortcomings and feel miserable, that is not enough. You haven't yet found your true self as a child of God. To practice self-reflection, it is important to first realize that there is a wonderful and radiant nature deep within you. Then, you need to remove the dirt that is covering it. One of the methods for removing this dirt is the Eightfold Path. I have taught about it in a simple and modern way (see Chapter Two of *The Laws of the Sun* and *The True Eightfold Path*).

Right View—to have a balanced view of yourself

First is Right View or seeing rightly. I am sure you all have experienced in your daily lives how difficult it is even to "see" correctly. There are times when the way you see yourself might be different from how others see you or when the way you see somebody might be different from how they see themselves, and you can live for years without being aware of these gaps in perception. For example, a person may see himself or herself as worthless, despite the praise they receive from others. This means this person does not see rightly. The opposite is also true. Some people overestimate their own abilities and do not realize the critical views others have of them. So you need to understand how fixed and unadaptable your viewpoint is. You must try to look at things from various standpoints outside of yourself. Overestimating yourself can cause you to fall, but underestimating yourself is also wrong. Seeing yourself rightly is more important than anything else.

To see yourself rightly, you need a balanced view. You must understand that everyone sees differently. Even if someone speaks ill of you, there will be others who think well of you. This way of thinking can work as a safety net in your life. People tend to adopt an "all-or-nothing" attitude and think they are either totally loved or totally hated. It sways from one extreme to the other. It is important to understand that how you see things is not necessarily true.

Right Thought—correcting your thought

The Eightfold Path also includes the practice of thinking rightly. This is difficult, but it is the starting point. Why so? This is because many people today are not aware that what they think determines who they are. Many people identify themselves by their social status, the name given by their parents, their academic background, or the company they work for. Some identify themselves by the positive remarks they receive from others. However, this is not who they are.

The Roman philosopher and emperor Marcus Aurelius wrote in *Meditations* that a man's thoughts reveal who he is. Later, the American author, poet, and philosopher of New Thought Ralph Waldo Emerson made this idea popular. In the field of psychology, they also teach the idea, "what you think is who you are." This is true. In the other world, where everyone will go after death, there is nothing but thought; what you actually think is who you are. Essentially, you do not have physical attributes such as hands, legs, or mouth. You have them because you think that is you. But you actually don't have them. You don't have a brain or teeth either. You have nothing but your thoughts; you are thought itself.

Through the eternal cycle of reincarnation, we are polishing our souls. But what we are polishing is our thoughts. So if you can master thinking rightly, you have completed about 80 percent of your spiritual discipline in this lifetime.

However, most people have not paid attention to their thoughts, nor are they even aware that they are actually thinking. They live each day without thinking about their thoughts, and only their fleeting thoughts flash through their heads. Please think about it. Before lunchtime, you think about what you will eat for lunch; after a meal, you think about how sleepy you feel; when you feel sleepy, you think about making coffee. Don't you have such random feelings or thoughts passing through your head? If you are such a person, it means you do not really understand what thinking is.

In a day, your mind actively thinks for at least 16 hours while you are awake. In those 16 hours, what do you think about? What kind of thoughts have you had? Have you ever stopped to think about it? What has been in your mind for those 16 hours? Did you have zero thoughts? Maybe you felt some emotions? Perhaps, for the majority of the time, you were concerned about some kind of personal problem. Your thoughts may be stuck on one particular worry, such as money, your parents, school, job, or your superiors at work. You may have spent all day, all 16 hours, worrying about that one problem. Is this the right way to use your time? Is it right to waste your time like this? If you are what you are thinking about, is it right to leave it as it is? It should not be.

One important method of self-reflection is to examine your thoughts. Each day you need to set aside some time to examine the thoughts you have had during that day. Since you woke up in the morning, what did you think of? What kind of thoughts popped into your mind? Was your mind empty? Were they useless thoughts? These are some points you should check.

If you find that your 16 hours have been filled with noble thoughts after reflecting on your thoughts, your soul is highly refined. If your thoughts have been filled with love, you are extraordinary. Also, you are an extraordinary person if your thoughts are filled with compassion. Have you ever checked on your thoughts in this way? I want you to check them sometimes. The thoughts you discover are you yourself. If you look back on the thoughts you had throughout the day and find that they were negative and dirty, then this is who you are.

But once again, you should not adopt an all-or-nothing attitude. Everyone has all kinds of thoughts throughout the day. As long as you are human, it's natural. Whenever you think in the wrong way, you should try to remove those negative thoughts and change your mind. Those who can think only of positive thoughts are rare. It is not easy to always examine your thoughts as if they were in a transparent glass box. But if you can correct the negative thoughts that arise, your mind can be purified. Once you understand this process, it is essential to practice it every day.

6

Self-Reflection for Progress

Right Effort—the path from ordinary to extraordinary

In this lecture on the principle of progress, the main point I wanted to tell you is about "progress through the Middle Way." This is closely related to Right Effort and Right Will.

On many occasions, I have emphasized the importance of making an effort. And I will continue to do so. We have all started from the ordinary, and because we are ordinary, we need to make strenuous efforts every day. Even if you are ordinary, a path to becoming extraordinary will open up through constant daily effort. Even if you are slow, foolish, or mediocre, through the process of accumulation, you will be able to do what an extraordinary person can do. This is the belief I have lived with until today.

There are many intelligent people, smart people, and multitalented people, and in a matter of a year or two, they may acquire expertise in a particular field. However, if you are ordinary, why not aim to achieve the same results in 5 or 10 years like a tortoise? This world is full of gifted people. But I do not envy how they can master things in a shorter time. I acknowledge that I am ordinary, so I know I can achieve what takes them only a year in five years—if not five years, then maybe 10 years. As long as I spend ten times the amount of time, I believe I can always catch up to them. This is true in all things. And if I can enjoy the path or the process to my goal, this is the greatest happiness. It is also important to thank heavens for you not being smart because it means you have many things to learn. It makes studying more fun. It is all the more important to be grateful to God for not making you clever because it means you have a lot of potentials to grow. This is one way of understanding the path of the Right Effort.

Right Will—realizing a great ideal as God's volunteer

Next, I would like to explain Right Will, which means to use our willpower in the right way. This is important. It is closely connected to self-realization. How you hold on to your ideals and how you realize them—these are where many problems lie and are the secret to your success in life.

Self-realization is a popular theme today; you may already be studying it through other books or seminars in the world today. However, the aim of most theories on self-realization seems to be on achieving worldly success or winning the admiration of others. The new set of values that you have been studying at Happy Science through books of Truth, lectures, and seminars embodies the perspective of God and the high spirits. Once you know these Truths, you should aim for true self-realization that accords with God's will rather than with superficial worldly success. Never neglect this point.

More and more people are joining Happy Science, and many of them say that they want to help us in our work of conveying the Truth. Many people are very cooperative. However, there can be a mistake in this. I accept your passion. I accept your ideals. I accept your willingness. But you must not convey the Truth for the sake of fulfilling your personal desire. You cannot. Remember that you are doing it to realize God's ideals. Remember that you are "volunteers" aiming to realize God's ideals. I did not start this movement to realize my own goals. I started it to realize God's ideals as God's volunteer. It is good to have high ideals or goals, but when you pursue them, do not do so from a mistaken standpoint. You must not take advantage of Happy Science and the Truth for your self-realization or to make a name for yourself in this world. This is a mistake. This is wrong. First, there are God's ideals; then, there is a great river that flows toward God's ideals. Your role is that of a single drop of water in this river. You must never forget this.

7

Love, Prayer, and Self-realization

Therefore, using and maintaining Right Will is the principle to succeed and progress in life, and the ultimate aim of progress is to embody God's will. This is also the ultimate aim of love. Always remember this. In this sense, you are allowed to pray for your self-realization. You can pray so that you can progress in the right way. Your prayers should not only be for your own happiness; rather, you should set your ultimate ideals as God's ideals and pray, "May I be close to God's ideals. O high spirits, please guide me to be God's servant." Do not make this mistake. You must never make this mistake. Strive for true self-realization and a true success by practicing love and prayer in the right way.

God is the ultimate form of love. We are all on this path of the developmental stages of love. We live in love; love is everything—love is life, love is light, love is energy, and love is a great river and we are living in this river. Be aware that we are in a vast ocean of love; this awareness is the basis for praying to realize great ideals. I would like you to understand the true meaning of the sequence, "from love to prayer, then from prayer to self-realization."

You must begin by making a constant effort to reflect on yourself, establish a strong self, and enter the Middle Way. Through this effort, you will awaken to infinite love and prayer, and a path to true success will open up before you. Every day, even I am walking on this path, so let us walk together and do our best together.

Afterword to The Principle of Happiness

I want a million people to share the same aspiration as me. I truly wish so. The past four years have shown that the Principle of Happiness that I advocate are the pathway to true salvation. With this validation as a foundation, I want to launch a great movement for human salvation from this land, Japan.

I want to carry out this movement for human happiness with you, the readers of this book. I want to eradicate atheism and harmful spiritual activities from society and establish pillars of Truth in this land. I want this Truth to be known by as many people as possible and to usher in the dawn of a new era.

You, who have found this book, awaken! You are one of the leaders in this age of salvation.

Ryuho Okawa
Master & CEO of Happy Science Group
September 1990

Afterword to The Principle of Enlightenment

The principle of enlightenment, the principle of progress, and the principle of wisdom, which play pivotal roles in the Laws, are taught in this book. These principles are the compass of the mind, so if you are undergoing spiritual training based on the Truth, you cannot live without them. Being strict with yourself and being steady prevents souls from falling as they advance, while also maintaining harmony with other people.

In particular, the idea of progress through the Middle Way and the developmental stages of wisdom will promise the eternal advancement of your soul.

Ryuho Okawa
Master & CEO of Happy Science Group
October 1990

Afterword to the newly revised first volume of
The Ten Principles from El Cantare

This book shows readers how I started off as a religious leader.

These fervent lectures created passionate members all across the country.

When I reread this book, I feel I can pat myself on the back for giving it my all in my teens and twenties also.

My sincerity; the passionate pursuit of the Truth without the fear of loneliness; the challenge of studying a vast number of books. When I look back over the past 30 years and think about how I never drowned in love in my private life but lived for the love of the public (world), I can assert that I have no regrets in my life.

The path to the future is still long and my battle will continue.

Ryuho Okawa
Master & CEO of Happy Science Group
July 26, 2020

ABOUT THE AUTHOR

RYUHO OKAWA was born on July 7th 1956, in Tokushima, Japan. After graduating from the University of Tokyo with a law degree, he joined a Tokyo-based trading house. While working at its New York headquarters, he studied international finance at the Graduate Center of the City University of New York. In 1981, he attained Great Enlightenment and became aware that he is El Cantare with a mission to bring salvation to all humankind. In 1986, he established Happy Science. It now has members in over 160 countries across the world, with more than 700 branches and temples as well as 10,000 missionary houses around the world. The total number of lectures has exceeded 3,350 (of which more than 150 are in English) and over 2,900 books (of which more than 600 are Spiritual Interview Series) have been published, many of which are translated into 37 languages. Many of the books, including *The Laws of the Sun* have become best sellers or million sellers. To date, Happy Science has produced 23 movies. The original story and original concept were given by the Executive Producer Ryuho Okawa. Recent movie titles are *Beautiful Lure—A Modern Tale of "Painted Skin"* (live-action, May 2021), *Into the Dreams...and Horror Experiences* (live-action, August 2021), and *The Laws of the Universe— The Age of Elohim* (animation movie, October 2021). He has also composed the lyrics and music of over 450 songs, such as theme songs and featured songs of movies. Moreover, he is the Founder of Happy Science University and Happy Science Academy (Junior and Senior High School), Founder and President of the Happiness Realization Party, Founder and Honorary Headmaster of Happy Science Institute of Government and Management, Founder of IRH Press Co., Ltd., and the Chairperson of NEW STAR PRODUCTION Co., Ltd. and ARI Production Co., Ltd.

WHAT IS EL CANTARE?

El Cantare means "the Light of the Earth," and is the Supreme God of the Earth who has been guiding humankind since the beginning of Genesis. He is whom Jesus called Father and Muhammad called Allah, and is the Creator in Shintoism, *Ame-no-Mioya-Gami*. Different parts of El Cantare's core consciousness have descended to Earth in the past, once as Alpha and another as Elohim. His branch spirits, such as Shakyamuni Buddha and Hermes, have descended to Earth many times and helped to flourish many civilizations. To unite various religions and to integrate various fields of study in order to build a new civilization on Earth, a part of the core consciousness has descended to Earth as Master Ryuho Okawa.

El Cantare,
God of the Earth

Ra Mu
17,000 years ago

Alpha
330 million
years ago

Elohim
150 million
years ago

Shakyamuni Buddha
2,600 years ago

Thoth
12,000 years ago

Hermes
4,300 years ago

Rient Arl Croud
7,000 years ago

Ophealis
6,500 years ago

Ryuho Okawa

Alpha is a part of the core consciousness of El Cantare who descended to Earth around 330 million years ago. Alpha preached Earth's Truths to harmonize and unify Earth-born humans and space people who came from other planets.

Elohim is a part of El Cantare's core consciousness who descended to Earth around 150 million years ago. He gave wisdom, mainly on the differences of light and darkness, good and evil.

Shakyamuni Buddha was born as a prince into the Shakya Clan in India around 2,600 years ago. When he was 29 years old, he renounced the world and sought enlightenment. He later attained Great Enlightenment and founded Buddhism.

Hermes is one of the 12 Olympian gods in Greek mythology, but the spiritual Truth is that he taught the teachings of love and progress around 4,300 years ago that became the origin of the current Western civilization. He is a hero that truly existed.

Ophealis was born in Greece around 6,500 years ago and was the leader who took an expedition to as far as Egypt. He is the God of miracles, prosperity, and arts, and is known as Osiris in the Egyptian mythology.

Rient Arl Croud was born as a king of the ancient Incan Empire around 7,000 years ago and taught about the mysteries of the mind. In the heavenly world, he is responsible for the interactions that take place between various planets.

Thoth was an almighty leader who built the golden age of the Atlantic civilization around 12,000 years ago. In the Egyptian mythology, he is known as god Thoth.

Ra Mu was a leader who built the golden age of the civilization of Mu around 17,000 years ago. As a religious leader and a politician, he ruled by uniting religion and politics.

ABOUT HAPPY SCIENCE

Happy Science is a global movement that empowers individuals to find purpose and spiritual happiness and to share that happiness with their families, societies, and the world. With more than 12 million members around the world, Happy Science aims to increase awareness of spiritual truths and expand our capacity for love, compassion, and joy so that together we can create the kind of world we all wish to live in.

Activities at Happy Science are based on the Principle of Happiness (Love, Wisdom, Self-Reflection, and Progress). This principle embraces worldwide philosophies and beliefs, transcending boundaries of culture and religions.

Love teaches us to give ourselves freely without expecting anything in return; it encompasses giving, nurturing, and forgiving.

Wisdom leads us to the insights of spiritual truths, and opens us to the true meaning of life and the will of God (the universe, the highest power, Buddha).

Self-Reflection brings a mindful, nonjudgmental lens to our thoughts and actions to help us find our truest selves—the essence of our souls—and deepen our connection to the highest power. It helps us attain a clean and peaceful mind and leads us to the right life path.

Progress emphasizes the positive, dynamic aspects of our spiritual growth—actions we can take to manifest and spread happiness around the world. It's a path that not only expands our soul growth, but also furthers the collective potential of the world we live in.

PROGRAMS AND EVENTS

The doors of Happy Science are open to all. We offer a variety of programs and events, including self-exploration and self-growth programs, spiritual seminars, meditation and contemplation sessions, study groups, and book events.

Our programs are designed to:
* Deepen your understanding of your purpose and meaning in life
* Improve your relationships and increase your capacity to love unconditionally
* Attain peace of mind, decrease anxiety and stress, and feel positive
* Gain deeper insights and a broader perspective on the world
* Learn how to overcome life's challenges
    ... and much more.

For more information, visit <u>happy-science.org</u>.

CONTACT INFORMATION

Happy Science is a worldwide organization with faith centers around the globe. For a comprehensive list of centers, visit the worldwide directory at *happy-science.org*. The following are some of the many Happy Science locations:

UNITED STATES AND CANADA

New York
79 Franklin St., New York, NY 10013
Phone: 212-343-7972
Fax: 212-343-7973
Email: ny@happy-science.org
Website: happyscience-usa.org

New Jersey
725 River Rd, #102B, Edgewater, NJ 07020
Phone: 201-313-0127
Fax: 201-313-0120
Email: nj@happy-science.org
Website: happyscience-usa.org

Florida
5208 8th St., Zephyrhills, FL 33542
Phone: 813-715-0000
Fax: 813-715-0010
Email: florida@happy-science.org
Website: happyscience-usa.org

Atlanta
1874 Piedmont Ave., NE Suite 360-C
Atlanta, GA 30324
Phone: 404-892-7770
Email: atlanta@happy-science.org
Website: happyscience-usa.org

San Francisco
525 Clinton St.
Redwood City, CA 94062
Phone & Fax: 650-363-2777
Email: sf@happy-science.org
Website: happyscience-usa.org

Los Angeles
1590 E. Del Mar Blvd., Pasadena, CA 91106
Phone: 626-395-7775
Fax: 626-395-7776
Email: la@happy-science.org
Website: happyscience-usa.org

Orange County
10231 Slater Ave., #204
Fountain Valley, CA 92708
Phone: 714-659-1501
Email: oc@happy-science.org
Website: happyscience-usa.org

San Diego
7841 Balboa Ave., Suite #202
San Diego, CA 92111
Phone: 626-395-7775
Fax: 626-395-7776
E-mail: sandiego@happy-science.org
Website: happyscience-usa.org

Hawaii
Phone: 808-591-9772
Fax: 808-591-9776
Email: hi@happy-science.org
Website: happyscience-usa.org

Kauai
3343 Kanakolu Street, Suite 5
Lihue, HI 96766, U.S.A.
Phone: 808-822-7007
Fax: 808-822-6007
Email: kauai-hi@happy-science.org
Website: happyscience-usa.org

Toronto
845 The Queensway
Etobicoke ON M8Z 1N6 Canada
Phone: 1-416-901-3747
Email: toronto@happy-science.org
Website: happy-science.ca

Vancouver
#201-2607 East 49th Avenue
Vancouver, BC, V5S 1J9, Canada
Phone: 1-604-437-7735
Fax: 1-604-437-7764
Email: vancouver@happy-science.org
Website: happy-science.ca

INTERNATIONAL

Tokyo
1-6-7 Togoshi, Shinagawa
Tokyo, 142-0041 Japan
Phone: 81-3-6384-5770
Fax: 81-3-6384-5776
Email: tokyo@happy-science.org
Website: happy-science.org

Seoul
74, Sadang-ro 27-gil,
Dongjak-gu, Seoul, Korea
Phone: 82-2-3478-8777
Fax: 82-2-3478-9777
Email: korea@happy-science.org
Website: happyscience-korea.org

London
3 Margaret St.
London,W1W 8RE United Kingdom
Phone: 44-20-7323-9255
Fax: 44-20-7323-9344
Email: eu@happy-science.org
Website: happyscience-uk.org

Taipei
No. 89, Lane 155, Dunhua N. Road
Songshan District, Taipei City 105, Taiwan
Phone: 886-2-2719-9377
Fax: 886-2-2719-5570
Email: taiwan@happy-science.org
Website: happyscience-tw.org

Sydney
516 Pacific Hwy, Lane Cove North,
NSW 2066, Australia
Phone: 61-2-9411-2877
Fax: 61-2-9411-2822
Email: sydney@happy-science.org

Malaysia
No 22A, Block 2, Jalil Link Jalan Jalil
Jaya 2, Bukit Jalil 57000, Kuala Lumpur, Malaysia
Phone: 60-3-8998-7877
Fax: 60-3-8998-7977
Email: malaysia@happy-science.org
Website: happyscience.org.my

Brazil Headquarters
Rua. Domingos de Morais 1154,
Vila Mariana, Sao Paulo SP
CEP 04010-100, Brazil
Phone: 55-11-5088-3800
Email: sp@happy-science.org
Website: happyscience.com.br

Nepal
Kathmandu Metropolitan City Ward
No. 15,
Ring Road, Kimdol,
Sitapaila Kathmandu, Nepal
Phone: 97-714-272931
Email: nepal@happy-science.org

Jundiai
Rua Congo, 447, Jd. Bonfiglioli
Jundiai-CEP, 13207-340
Phone: 55-11-4587-5952
Email: jundiai@happy-science.org

Uganda
Plot 877 Rubaga Road, Kampala
P.O. Box 34130, Kampala, Uganda
Phone: 256-79-4682-121
Email: uganda@happy-science.org
Website: happyscience-uganda.org

The Happiness Realization Party (HRP) was founded in May 2009 by Master Ryuho Okawa as part of the Happy Science Group. HRP strives to improve the Japanese society, based on three basic political principles of "freedom, democracy, and faith," and let Japan promote individual and public happiness from Asia to the world as a leader nation.

1) Diplomacy and Security: Protecting Freedom, Democracy, and Faith of Japan and the World from China's Totalitarianism

Japan's current defense system is insufficient against China's expanding hegemony and the threat of North Korea's nuclear missiles. Japan, as the leader of Asia, must strengthen its defense power and promote strategic diplomacy together with the nations which share the values of freedom, democracy, and faith. Further, HRP aims to realize world peace under the leadership of Japan, the nation with the spirit of religious tolerance.

2) Economy: Early economic recovery through utilizing the "wisdom of the private sector"

Economy has been damaged severely by the novel coronavirus originated in China. Many companies have been forced into bankruptcy or out of business. What is needed for economic recovery now is not subsidies and regulations by the government, but policies which can utilize the "wisdom of the private sector."

For more information, visit en.hr-party.jp

HAPPY SCIENCE ACADEMY JUNIOR AND SENIOR HIGH SCHOOL

Happy Science Academy Junior and Senior High School is a boarding school founded with the goal of educating the future leaders of the world who can have a big vision, persevere, and take on new challenges.

Currently, there are two campuses in Japan; the Nasu Main Campus in Tochigi Prefecture, founded in 2010, and the Kansai Campus in Shiga Prefecture, founded in 2013.

Nasu Main Campus

Kansai Campus

H͟S͟U͟ HAPPY SCIENCE UNIVERSITY

THE FOUNDING SPIRIT AND THE GOAL OF EDUCATION

Based on the founding philosophy of the university, "Exploration of happiness and the creation of a new civilization," education, research and studies will be provided to help students acquire deep understanding grounded in religious belief and advanced expertise with the objectives of producing "great talents of virtue" who can contribute in a broad-ranging way to serve Japan and the international society.

FACULTIES

Faculty of human happiness

Students in this faculty will pursue liberal arts from various perspectives with a multidisciplinary approach, explore and envision an ideal state of human beings and society.

Faculty of successful management

This faculty aims to realize successful management that helps organizations to create value and wealth for society and to contribute to the happiness and the development of management and employees as well as society as a whole.

Faculty of future creation

Students in this faculty study subjects such as political science, journalism, performing arts and artistic expression, and explore and present new political and cultural models based on truth, goodness and beauty.

Faculty of future industry

This faculty aims to nurture engineers who can resolve various issues facing modern civilization from a technological standpoint and contribute to the creation of new industries of the future.

ABOUT IRH PRESS

IRH Press Co., Ltd., based in Tokyo, was founded in 1987 as a publishing division of Happy Science. IRH Press publishes religious and spiritual books, journals, magazines and also operates broadcast and film production enterprises. For more information, visit *okawabooks.com*.

Follow us on:

Facebook: Okawa Books

Twitter: Okawa Books

Goodreads: Ryuho Okawa

Instagram: OkawaBooks

Pinterest: Okawa Books

--------- **NEWSLETTER** ---------

To receive book related news, promotions and events, please subscribe to our newsletter below.

https://okawabooks.us11.list-manage.com/subscribe?u=1fc70960eefd92668052a
b7f8&id=2fbd8150ef

--------- **MEDIA** ---------

OKAWA BOOK CLUB

A conversation about Ryuho Okawa's titles, topics ranging from self-help, current affairs, spirituality and religions.

Available at iTunes, Spotify and Amazon Music.

Apple iTunes:

https://podcasts.apple.com/us/podcast/okawa-book-club/id1527893043

Spotify:

https://open.spotify.com/show/09mpgX2iJ6stVm4eBRdo2b

Amazon Music:

https://music.amazon.com/podcasts/7b759f24-ff72-4523-bfee-24f48294998f/
Okawa-Book-Club

BOOKS BY RYUHO OKAWA

RYUHO OKAWA'S LAWS SERIES

The Laws Series is an annual volume of books that are mainly comprised of Ryuho Okawa's lectures that function as universal guidance to all people. They are of various topics that were given in accordance with the changes that each year brings. *The Laws of the Sun*, the first publication of the laws series, ranked in the annual best-selling list in Japan in 1994. Since, the laws series' titles have ranked in the annual best-selling list every year for more than two decades, setting socio-cultural trends in Japan and around the world.

The 27th Laws Series
THE LAWS OF SECRET

AWAKEN TO THIS NEW WORLD
AND CHANGE YOUR LIFE

Paperback • 248 pages • $16.95
ISBN: 978-1-942125-81-5

Our physical world coexists with the multi-dimensional spirit world and we are constantly interacting with some kind of spiritual energy, whether positive or negative, without consciously realizing it. This book reveals how our lives are affected by invisible influences, including the spiritual reasons behind influenza, the novel coronavirus infection, and other illnesses.

The new view of the world in this book will inspire you to change your life in a better direction, and to become someone who can give hope and courage to others in this age of confusion.

*For a complete list of books, visit **okawabooks.com***

THE TRILOGY

The first three volumes of the Laws Series, *The Laws of the Sun*, *The Golden Laws*, and *The Nine Dimensions* make a trilogy that completes the basic framework of the teachings of God's Truths. *The Laws of the Sun* discusses the structure of God's Laws, *The Golden Laws* expounds on the doctrine of time, and *The Nine Dimensions* reveals the nature of space.

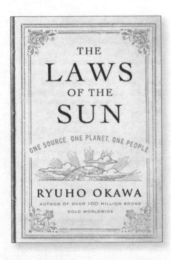

THE LAWS OF THE SUN

ONE SOURCE, ONE PLANET,
ONE PEOPLE

Paperback • 288 pages • $15.95
ISBN: 978-1-942125-43-3

IMAGINE IF YOU COULD ASK GOD why He created this world and what spiritual laws He used to shape us—and everything around us. If we could understand His designs and intentions, we could discover what our goals in life should be and whether our actions move us closer to those goals or farther away.

At a young age, a spiritual calling prompted Ryuho Okawa to outline what he innately understood to be universal truths for all humankind. In *The Laws of the Sun*, Okawa outlines these laws of the universe and provides a road map for living one's life with greater purpose and meaning.

In this powerful book, Ryuho Okawa reveals the transcendent nature of consciousness and the secrets of our multidimensional universe and our place in it. By understanding the different stages of love and following the Buddhist Eightfold Path, he believes we can speed up our eternal process of development. *The Laws of the Sun* shows the way to realize true happiness—a happiness that continues from this world through the other.

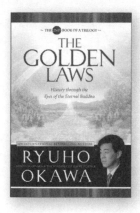

THE GOLDEN LAWS

HISTORY THROUGH THE EYES OF THE ETERNAL BUDDHA

Paperback • 201 pages • $14.95
ISBN: 978-1-941779-81-1

Throughout history, Great Guiding Spirits have been present on Earth in both the East and the West at crucial points in human history to further our spiritual development. *The Golden Laws* reveals how Divine Plan has been unfolding on Earth, and outlines 5,000 years of the secret history of humankind. Once we understand the true course of history, through past, present and into the future, we cannot help but become aware of the significance of our spiritual mission in the present age.

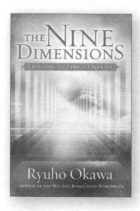

THE NINE DIMENSIONS

UNVEILING THE LAWS OF ETERNITY

Paperback • 168 pages • $15.95
ISBN: 978-0-982698-56-3

This book is a window into the mind of our loving God, who designed this world and the vast, wondrous world of our afterlife as a school with many levels through which our souls learn and grow. When the religions and cultures of the world discover the truth of their common spiritual origin, they will be inspired to accept their differences, come together under faith in God, and build an era of harmony and peaceful progress on Earth.

*For a complete list of books, visit **okawabooks.com***

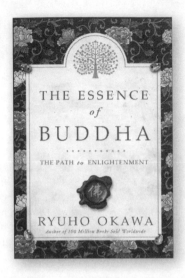

The Essence of Buddha

THE PATH TO ENLIGHTENMENT

Paperback • 208 pages • $14.95
ISBN: 978-1-942125-06-8

In this book, Ryuho Okawa imparts in simple and accessible language his wisdom about the essence of Shakyamuni Buddha's philosophy of life and enlightenment–teachings that have been inspiring people all over the world for over 2,500 years. By offering a new perspective on core Buddhist thoughts that have long been cloaked in mystique, Okawa brings these teachings to life for modern people. *The Essence of Buddha* distills a way of life that anyone can practice to achieve a life of self-growth, compassionate living, and true happiness.

---

*For a complete list of books, visit **okawabooks.com***

THE TRUE EIGHTFOLD PATH

GUIDEPOSTS FOR SELF-INNOVATION

Paperback • 256 pages • $16.95
ISBN: 978-1-942125-80-8

This book explains how we can apply the Eightfold Path, one of the main pillars of Shakyamuni Buddha's teachings, as everyday guideposts in the modern-age to achieve self-innovation to live better and make positive changes in these uncertain times.

THE CHALLENGE OF THE MIND

AN ESSENTIAL GUIDE TO BUDDHA'S TEACHINGS: ZEN, KARMA AND ENLIGHTENMENT

Paperback • 208 pages • $16.95
ISBN: 978-1-942125-45-7

In this book, Ryuho Okawa explains essential Buddhist tenets and how to put them into practice. Enlightenment is not just an abstract idea but one that everyone can experience to some extent. Okawa offers a solid basis of reason and intellectual understanding to Buddhist concepts. By applying these basic principles to our lives, we can direct our minds to higher ideals and create a bright future for ourselves and others.

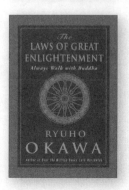

THE LAWS OF GREAT ENLIGHTENMENT

ALWAYS WALK WITH BUDDHA

Paperback • 232 pages • $17.95
ISBN: 978-1-942125-62-4

Constant self-blame for mistakes, setbacks, or failures and feelings of unforgivingness toward others are hard to overcome. Through the power of enlightenment we can learn to forgive ourselves and others, overcome life's problems, and courageously create a brighter future ourselves. This book addresses the core problems of life that people often struggle with and offers advice on how to overcome them based on spiritual truths.

For a complete list of books, visit **okawabooks.com**

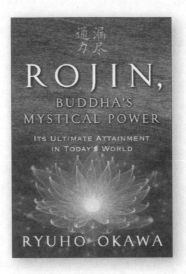

Rojin, Buddha's Mystical Power

ITS ULTIMATE ATTAINMENT IN TODAY'S WORLD

Paperback • 224 pages • $16.95
ISBN: 978-1-942125-82-2

In this book, Ryuho Okawa has redefined the traditional Buddhist term *Rojin* and explained that in modern society it means the following: the ability for individuals with great spiritual powers to live in the world as people with common sense while using their abilities to the optimal level. This book will unravel the mystery of the mind and lead you to the path to enlightenment.

---

*For a complete list of books, visit **okawabooks.com***

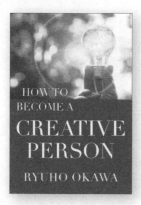

HOW TO BECOME A CREATIVE PERSON

HOW CAN WE BECOME CREATIVE WHEN WE FEEL WE ARE NOT NATURALLY CREATIVE?

Paperback • 176 pages • $16.95
ISBN: 978-1-942125-84-6

How can we become creative when we feel we are not naturally creative? This book provides easy to follow universal and hands-on-rules to become a creative person in work and life. These methods of becoming creative are certain to bring you success in work and life. Discover the secret ingredient for becoming truly creative.

Scheduled to be published in Spring of 2022.

THE TEN PRINCIPLES FROM EL CANTARE VOLUME II

RYUHO OKAWA'S FIRST LECTURES ON HIS WISH TO SAVE THE WORLD

Paperback • 272 pages • $16.95
ISBN: 978-1-942125-86-0

A sequel to *The Ten Principles from El Cantare Volume I*. Volume II reveals the Creator's three major inventions; the secret of the creation of human souls, the meaning of time, and 'happiness' as life's purpose. By reading this book, you can not only improve yourself but learn how to make differences in society and create an ideal, utopian world.

*For a complete list of books, visit **okawabooks.com***

RECOMMENDED BOOKS

THE STRONG MIND

THE ART OF BUILDING THE INNER STRENGTH
TO OVERCOME LIFE'S DIFFICULTIES

Paperback • 192 pages • $15.95
ISBN: 978-1-942125-36-5

The strong mind is what we need to rise time and again, and to move forward no matter what difficulties we face in life. This book will inspire and empower you to take courage, develop a mature and cultivated heart, and achieve resilience and hardiness so that you can break through the barriers of your limits and keep winning in the battle of your life.

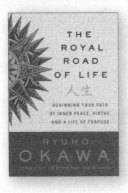

THE ROYAL ROAD OF LIFE

BEGINNING YOUR PATH OF INNER PEACE,
VIRTUE, AND A LIFE OF PURPOSE

Paperback • 224 pages • $16.95
ISBN: 978-1-942125-53-2

With over 30 years of lectures and teachings spanning diverse topics of faith, self-growth, leadership (and more), Ryuho Okawa presents the profound eastern wisdom that he has cultivated on his approach to life. The Royal Road of Life illuminates a path to becoming a person of virtue, whose character and depth will move and inspire others towards the same meaningful destination.

THE POWER OF BASICS

INTRODUCTION TO MODERN ZEN LIFE OF CALM,
SPIRITUALITY AND SUCCESS

Paperback • 232 pages • $16.95
ISBN:978-1-942125-75-4

The power of basics is a necessary asset to excel at any kind of work. It is the power to meticulously pursue tasks with a quiet Zen mindset. If you master this power of basics, you can achieve new levels of productivity regardless of your profession, and attain new heights of success and happiness. This book also describes the essence of an intellectual life, thereby reviving the true spirit of Zen in the modern age.

*For a complete list of books, visit **okawabooks.com***

THE LAWS SERIES

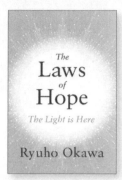

THE LAWS OF HOPE

THE LIGHT IS HERE

Paperback • 224 pages • $16.95
ISBN:978-1-942125-76-1

This book provides ways to bring light and hope to ourselves through our own efforts, even in the midst of sufferings and adversities. Inspired by a wish to bring happiness, success, and hope to humanity, Okawa shows us how to look at and think about our lives and circumstances. He says that hopes come true when we have the right mindset inside us.

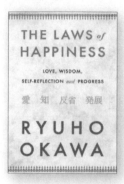

THE LAWS OF HAPPINESS

LOVE, WISDOM, SELF-REFLECTION AND PROGRESS

Paperback • 264 pages • $16.95
ISBN: 978-1-942125-70-9

What is happiness? In this book, Ryuho Okawa explains that happiness is not found outside us; it's found within us, in how we think, how we look at our lives in this world, what we believe in, and how we devote our hearts to the work we do. Even as we go through suffering and unfavorable circumstances, we can always shift our mindset and become happier by simply *giving love* instead of *taking love*.

THE LAWS OF SUCCESS

A SPIRITUAL GUIDE TO TURNING
YOUR HOPES INTO REALITY

Paperback • 208 pages • $15.95
ISBN: 978-1-942125-15-0

The Laws of Success offers 8 spiritual principles that, when put to practice in our day-to-day life, will help us attain lasting success. The timeless wisdom and practical steps that Ryuho Okawa offers will guide us through any difficulties and problems we may face in life, and serve as guiding principles for living a positive, constructive, and meaningful life.

For a complete list of books, visit **okawabooks.com**

THE LAWS OF FAITH
One World Beyond Differences

THE ART OF INFLUENCE
28 Ways to Win People's Hearts and
Bring Positive Change to Your Life

THE HELL YOU NEVER KNEW
And How to Avoid Going There

TWICEBORN
My Early Thoughts that Revealed My True Mission

WORRY-FREE LIVING
Let Go of Stress and Live in Peace and Happiness

THE REAL EXORCIST
Attain Wisdom to Conquer Evil

MY JOURNEY THROUGH THE SPIRIT WORLD
A True Account of My Experiences of the Hereafter

THE HEART OF WORK
10 Keys to Living Your Calling

HEALING FROM WITHIN
Life-Changing Keys to Calm, Spiritual, and Healthy Living

MUSICS BY RYUHO OKAWA

THE THUNDER

a composition for repelling the Coronavirus

We have been granted this music from our Lord. It will repel away the novel Coronavirus originated in China. Experience this magnificent powerful music.

Search on YouTube

the thunder coronavirus for a short ad!

THE EXORCISM

prayer music for repelling Lost Spirits

Feel the divine vibrations of this Japanese and Western exorcising symphony to banish all evil possessions you suffer from and to purify your space!

Search on YouTube

the exorcism repelling for a short ad!